FIFTY KEY WORDS: THE CHURCH

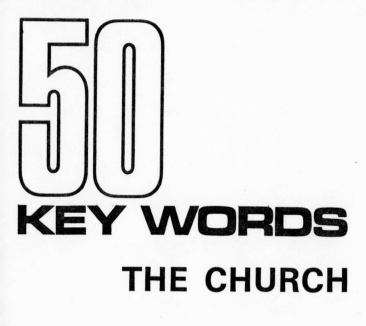

50
KEY WORDS
THE CHURCH

.by
WILLIAM STEWART

DISCARD

UNITY SCHOOL LIBRARY
UNITY VILLAGE, MISSOURI 64065

**JOHN KNOX PRESS
RICHMOND, VIRGINIA**

COPYRIGHT © 1970 LUTTERWORTH PRESS

LUTTERWORTH PRESS
4 BOUVERIE STREET, LONDON, E.C.4

JOHN KNOX PRESS
RICHMOND, VIRGINIA

STANDARD BOOK NUMBER: 8042-3891-X
LIBRARY OF CONGRESS CATALOG CARD NUMBER: 79-82935

PRINTED IN GREAT BRITAIN

LIST OF WORDS

INTRODUCTION

It is hoped that the brief articles which follow will be of help to the interested reader who suspects that a word, often familiar enough in itself, carries a wider, or different, shade of meaning in circles other than his own. While the writer naturally sees the picture from within his own tradition, an attempt has been made, within the limits of such articles, to point out such varieties of significance. In most instances it has seemed desirable to indicate something of the scriptural background of the words as well as their historical development.

Many of the key words on the Church are closely intertwined, and this has rendered inevitable a certain amount of repetition. Cross-references to some of the other relevant articles are indicated by giving their numbers at the end of the articles. The index shows where words not separately treated may be followed up, and a reading of the whole book should form some kind of introduction to a study of the various questions involved in the development of the Church and its Ministry.

No attempt has been made to document most of the references, apart from those from scripture which, unless otherwise stated, are from the RSV; but those interested may find it useful to refer to the writer's earlier book, *The Nature and Calling of the Church* (Madras, 1958), which has fairly full references to literature on the subject, as well as to World Council (Faith and Order) publications of more recent date.

While entirely responsible for what is lacking in this book, the writer would like to acknowledge most warmly the help given by the Rt. Rev. Bishop Michael Hollis, especially in the early stages of selection and planning, and by the Rev. J. W. Stevenson, D.D., Dunblane, who read and commented on many of the draft articles. William Stewart

ABSOLUTION: This word, signifying release from guilt and its disabling power, is used for the act in which such release is authoritatively declared. The authority was given by the risen Christ: 'If you forgive the sins of any, they are forgiven; if you retain the sins of any, they are retained' (John 20: 23). Comparing these words with Matt. 18: 18 and noting that in the Upper Room Luke records the presence of others besides the apostles (Luke 24: 33) this authority would appear to be given to the Church. Paul certainly directs the Church to discipline an erring brother and to restore the penitent (1 Cor. 5: 4f; 2 Cor. 2: 5–11). In certain ordination services (e.g. the Anglican) John 20: 23 is quoted with the singular: 'Whose sins thou dost forgive . . .' but this does not imply an authority exercised independently of the Church, and certain liturgies express the function of the whole body, e.g. when congregation and officiant in turn use words like these: 'May almighty God have mercy upon thee, forgive thee thy sins . . .'.

The Preaching of the Gospel is a potent means of conveying Absolution, and indeed the 'power of the keys' (Matt. 16: 19) has been interpreted as applying solely to this office, though the Gospel Sacraments are usually recognized as means to the same end. However words of Absolution are commonly used in the course of public worship. These may be an authoritative reminder of God's pardon: '. . . He pardoneth and absolveth . . .' or a prayer: 'The almighty God grant unto you pardon . . .' or even a solemn declaration to the individual: 'I absolve thee . . .' Besides Absolution declared in public worship, Calvin is one of many who saw the need of the distressed individual: He wrote:

> Should this man lay open the secret wound of his soul to his pastor, and hear these words of the Gospel especially addressed to him, 'Son, be of good cheer, thy sins are forgiven thee . . .' his mind will feel secure.

Calvin wrote against a background of medieval practice in

which the conviction that a priest was the necessary instrument of pardon, coupled with a practice in which outward acts of penance were prescribed, initially to express repentance, had led to abuses (e.g. the sale of Indulgences) which were among the causes of the Reformation. Such abuses conflicted with earlier teaching, such as that of Peter the Lombard:

> God remits sins through Himself alone . . . the power of binding and loosing is the power of showing a man to be bound or loosed.
>
> (Quoted K. E. Kirk; *Vision of God*, p. 290)

Modern psychiatry recognizes unresolved tensions as being at the root of much mental and physical trouble, as of social conflict. 'Pastoral Counselling' is a Christian response to this need, which properly sees the root trouble to be alienation from God. To convey the assurance of an end to this alienation through Christ to the troubled in conscience, the sick and the dying is to bring Absolution, and is a vital part of the office of the Christian minister.

[4, 43]

2 **ADVENT:** This synonym for arrival is the name of the four-week period which leads to Christmas, the festival of Christ's birth. The keynote of this first season of the Christian year is Preparation and Expectancy. That it occurs in the northern winter does not reflect authentic information on the precise date of the birth, but a fitness is seen in the nearness to the winter solstice, the lighting of candles on successive Advent Sundays symbolizing a growing expectancy, like the lightening of the sky before dawn.

Such observances should not imply a 'cyclic' view of reality. Indeed, to date events by the Christian era, as from Christ's birth, recalls the N.T. emphasis on what happened once for all:

'When the time had fully come, God sent forth His Son' (Gal. 4: 4; cf. Heb. 1: 2; John 1: 14). The coming of Christ is a unique event.

Advent readings usually include O.T. passages which point to an expected, decisive act of God: the promise that the seed of the woman will 'bruise the head' of the serpent (Gen. 3: 15), promise of a prophet 'like Moses' (Deut. 18: 18), of a King like David and of the Lord who 'will suddenly come to his temple' (Mal. 3: 1). Of all this, and words like 'The people who walked in darkness have seen a great light' (Isa. 9: 2) the N.T. proclaims that 'all the promises of God find their Yes in Him' (2 Cor. 1: 20).

The Advent call to prepare for Christ's coming now is related to N.T. passages on His coming to particular people. He came on the lake to His disciples (Mark 6: 50), and in judgement to the temple (Mark 11: 15ff) and He stands at the door and knocks (Rev. 3: 20). All this, with the Johannine promise 'I will come to you' (John 14: 18) reminds us that we do not worship an absent Lord nor live by a fading memory. What happened at Bethlehem takes form and reality in every generation.

There remains the expectation of the second Advent, a final return of Christ, to which the N.T. gives testimony. There have always been those who let this expectation divert them from present responsibility who, like the first apostles, 'stand looking into heaven' (Acts 1: 11). Paul rebuked those who, for this reason, neglected obligations (2 Thess. 3: 10); but there have been many 'Adventists' who have read the Bible, especially Daniel and Revelation, as giving cryptic information about this event and the end of the world. This can belittle the decisive character of what has already happened. Also it flies in the face of Christ's reminder 'It is not for you to know times or seasons' (Acts 1: 7). Yet the Church may not neglect this aspect of N.T. hope which asserts that the end of things temporal is not a feeble petering out nor a disaster beyond God's control, but is in the hands of

Him who 'will come to be our Judge'. Meantime we are to fill the time in His service (Matt. 24: 46) especially in the proclamation of the Gospel to the ends of the earth (Matt. 24: 14).

3 **APOSTLE** (Apostolate, Apostolic): The phrase 'the twelve apostles' points to the group chosen by Christ 'to be with him, and to be sent out to preach . . .' (Mark 3: 14). In the Gospels their usual title is 'disciples' (followers and learners) but, being sent out, they become apostles, from the Greek word for 'sending'. They shared in the commission: 'As the Father has sent me, even so I send you' (John 20: 21). Their number, that of Israel's tribes, points to the Church as being the new, true Israel. For this reason the early Church felt bound to fill the gap caused by the apostasy of Judas, and Matthias was chosen.

The choice of Matthias is described in ways which make it clear that apostles were 'chosen witnesses' particularly of Christ's resurrection (Acts 1: 22; 10: 41). So also Paul maintains his apostleship: '. . . Am I not an apostle? Have I not seen Jesus our Lord?' (1 Cor. 9: 1). Paul's example, however, shows that the term was not confined to the twelve. Apart from an 'apostle' of one church (Epaphroditus, Phil. 2: 25) Barnabas is an apostle of Christ (Acts 14: 14) as are others of whom nothing else is known (Rom. 16: 7) and there are 'false apostles' (Rev. 2: 2). There are, however, no later additions and the N.T. regards them as the essential witnesses forming the very foundation of the Church (Eph. 2: 20).

The apostles' authority was not in themselves but in their testimony (1 Cor. 15: 11). To the Galatians Paul writes that if even he himself or an angel from heaven should preach another Gospel, he is to be repudiated (Gal. 1: 8). The fact that Peter was rebuked not only by Christ but by Paul underlines the fact that the apostle is not the master of his message, but is subject to it.

4

The apostles had a key role in upbuilding the churches, visiting and confirming them (Acts 8 : 14), travelling to strengthen them (Acts 9 : 32; 14 : 21f) and writing to them. But they made no claim to 'lord it over' them (2 Cor. 1 : 24) and in corporate decisions had other counsellors (Acts 11 : 1).

Later Churches valued traditions of having been founded by apostles, and confidence that their bishops had been authorized by a sequence of consecrations from the apostles led to a theory of apostolic succession important both in the Roman Church, which joins it with belief in Peter's association with Rome, and in other episcopal Churches. Later bishops were not, of course, themselves witnesses of the Resurrection, but writers like Irenaeus indicate their functions as including the preservation of the purity of the apostolic faith. In the second century the test sought to be applied to determine which books should have a place in the Canon was that of whether or not they were apostolic in origin. These books, forming the N.T., became the touchstone for doctrinal statements, including the Creeds.

Apostolicity, as a note of the Church acknowledged in the Nicene Creed, implies (i) organic continuity with the Church founded on the Apostles, (ii) faithfulness to the Gospel 'once for all delivered to the saints' (Jude 3) and (iii) the continued 'sending' into the world with a mission from Christ. This last involving the whole Church, is seen to call for a 'lay apostolate' emphasized in Vatican II.

[4, 17, 24]

AUTHORITY: A Political Authority may enact rules and enforce compliance by sanctions. Though subject to limits (Acts 5 : 29) this is seen in the N.T. as according to God's will (Rom. 13 : 1). A Learned Authority is a master of his subject, whose statements are to be treated with respect, though subject to verification. In Morals there are various theories of ultimate authority, but for Christians moral verdicts are bound up with the Faith.

Jesus is said to have had authority unlike the Scribes whose teaching rested on others (Matt. 7: 29). Its self-authenticating nature is confirmed by His refusal to state His authority to cleanse the temple (Matt. 21: 27). His Ascension shows His continued authority in heaven and on earth (Matt. 28: 18; Phil. 2: 10).

Authority in the Church derives from Christ its 'only King and Head'. He is recorded as having authorized His disciples to preach, teach, heal and pronounce forgiveness in His name. Such authority, especially for the apostles (2 Cor. 10: 8; but cf. 2: 5–10) is exercised (i) in organizing and ordering churches and (ii) in determining whether or not teachings are in harmony with the Gospel. The N.T., as enshrining the authentic record of apostolic teaching, has retained decisive authority in the Church.

After Constantine, the way opened to enforce ecclesiastical obedience by physical sanctions, even to the death sentence. That political and spiritual authority were thus confused has embittered much Church controversy.

Ecclesiastical Authority is exercised in two wide spheres: (a) that of organization and administration, including 'the power to decree rites or ceremonies' (Art. xx, BCP). Authorities here range from the hierarchical (Papal and Episcopal) through the more conciliar Presbyterian to the Congregational. (b) The determination of doctrine as a true exposition of the Gospel. While the authority of Scripture is generally acknowledged in the Churches, differences emerge as to the proper means, under Christ, for interpreting the Faith, and the relevance for this of Tradition. Here the R.C. Church claims high authority for the hierarchy, with the Pope as Supreme Pontiff at its head. Vatican II has strengthened the role of the College of Bishops but

6

reaffirms 'the supreme, full, immediate and universal authority over the care of souls' of the Pope, in keeping with the decree on the infallibility of his *ex cathedra* utterances adopted by Vatican I.

Churches of the Reformation generally acknowledged Church Authority 'in controversies of Faith', subject to the provision that 'it is not lawful for the Church to ordain anything that is contrary to God's Word written'. The more radical Reformation, on the other hand, sought a more exclusive dependence on the Holy Spirit's direct leading. That spiritual authority can be effective only with the free consent of the believer is today agreed, but since it is, none the less, believed that there is a Faith once delivered to the Saints (Jude 3) the Church seeks an authority which is not tyranny within a life of freedom which is not anarchy.

[42, 47, 50]

BAPTISM: With few exceptions, Baptism has been from N.T. times the Sacrament of Christian initiation (Acts 2: 41; cf. Matt. 28: 18ff).

Ritual washings, practised in many religions, were familiar in Jewish circles (John 2: 6) and both Proselyte Baptism and sectarian baptisms apparently preceded John's 'baptism of repentance' (Mark 1: 4). While the former recalled Israel's crossing of the Red Sea, John's anticipated the coming of the Messiah. He called for repentance and baptized Jew as well as Gentile. Identifying himself with those He came to save, Jesus submitted to this Baptism, but later saw His own Baptism in His Passion (Luke 12: 50). Christian Baptism, depending on Christ's death and resurrection, follows these and is thus distinct from that of John (Acts 19: 1–5).

N.T. Baptism is Baptism into Christ (Rom. 6: 3) and is said

7

to be 'in' or 'into' His name, the fuller trinitarian formula (Matt. 28: 19) spelling out the implications of His coming (Acts 2: 38; Gal. 3: 27). The words imply both the authority for the act, and the sphere into which one is baptized. Identification with Christ in His death and resurrection (Rom. 6: 4; Col. 2: 12) is incorporation into His body, the Church (1 Cor. 12: 13) and fulfils circumcision, the seal of incorporation under the old Covenant (Col. 2: 11f). It is the Sacrament of forgiveness (Acts 2: 38; 22: 16), of cleansing (Heb. 10: 22) and a new birth (John 3: 5; Rom. 6: 4; Titus 3: 5).

Proselyte Baptism was self-administered except for children and slaves. As Christian Baptism was administered to a person, this casts light on Jesus' word that we must become as children (Mark 10: 15) and Paul's description of himself as Christ's bondslave (Acts 9: 18; Phil. 1: 1). Some Churches recognize Baptism by any officiant, though normally (and in Reformed Churches exclusively) it is by an ordained minister.

Baptism is by immersion, affusion or sprinkling. The original Greek signifies immersion, which also dramatizes death and resurrection. Yet the word is also used for other washings (Mark 7: 4Mg.) and immersion would seem unlikely in certain N.T. instances (Acts 2: 41; 16: 33). Other modes are contemplated in the very early *Didache*. Affusion symbolizes the 'pouring out' of the Spirit, and biblical references to sprinkling (Ezek. 36: 25; Heb. 10: 22) are rich in association with 'cleansing' from sin.

Churches differ as to the appropriate mode of administration, and as to the proper recipient of Baptism. Some (particularly Baptists) hold personal confession of faith to be necessary, as in most N.T. instances (but see Acts 2: 39; 11: 14; 16: 15, 33; 1 Cor. 7: 14). Controversy is recorded from the end of the second century, when there was a tendency to see Baptism as itself conveying forgiveness. For sins after Baptism the proposed remedy was either Gnostic repetition of Baptism, postponement to one's death-bed, or practices of Penance. If, however, Baptism

8

declares what is by the grace of Christ alone, the problem is eased. Baptism recovers significance as the Sacrament of entry on a life of Repentance and Faith. Consequently it is understood that Infant Baptism is administered on the faith of the Church, of those who bring their children, and the expected faith by which the baptized all his days will 'lay hold on his baptism'.

[26, 44]

CALLING (Vocation): When Paul wrote: 'Consider your call, brethren . . .' (1 Cor. 1: 26) he used a theme common to both Testaments, namely that the very existence of the Church depends on the invitation, summons or call of God. That man has a special place in creation is due to a divine calling (Ps. 8: 5). That Israel was a holy people is due only to God's gracious purpose (Deut. 7: 8) who called them out of Egypt. Indeed the common Hebrew for 'congregation' (*qahal*) implies a summons.

The Gospels show Christ addressing a gracious call to men: 'Come to me, all who labour . . .' (Matt. 11: 28), and stating as the purpose of his coming 'not to call the righteous but sinners' (Mark 2: 17). The theme recurs in Peter's sermon at Pentecost: 'every one whom the Lord our God calls' (Acts 2: 39), and in Paul's recognition of Christians as those 'called to be saints' (Rom. 1: 7). Such a calling implies responsibility to live in a manner worthy of it (Eph. 4: 1) which includes service (cf. Jesus' invitation: '. . . take my yoke upon you . . .' (Matt. 11: 28f).

Later Christian teachings both recognize that the Christian life is a calling and that there is a divine vocation of the Church as a whole. Every 'high' doctrine of the Church, whatever the polity, be it hierarchical or stressing the 'gathered' congregation, is rooted in the belief that the Church's very being rests on a divine calling.

The Church's calling is complemented by the calling of particular persons for service. Abraham, Moses, Samuel are but

B

examples of key figures in the O.T. whose life's work is determined by their response to a call. Though the concept is once applied to Cyrus, called without his knowledge (Isa. 45: 4), normally the call receives a conscious, willing response. It is acknowledged in Isaiah's experience of being called by name (Isa. 43: 1). In the N.T., Jesus invites certain people to leave all and follow Him, and sends out those whom He has called to serve (Mark 3: 13). Paul, addressing his readers as 'called to be saints' (Rom. 1: 7) does so as one who is himself 'called ... to be an apostle' (Rom. 1: 1). Further, his discussion of certain marriage problems underlies later recognition that both celibacy and the married state may be adopted as a divine vocation (1 Cor. 7: 17), and his teaching on diversity of gifts (Rom. 12; 1 Cor. 12) shows how varied may be individual vocations.

In Church history, the concept tended to be limited to 'vocations' to the monastic life, the priesthood or missionary service, designated religious vocations. Luther recovered the sense of the vocation of every Christian to serve his neighbour, even to be 'a Christ to his neighbour'. This is in line with an emphasis retained by the Orthodox on Baptism as the ordination of every Christian to divine service, also with the current recovery of the insight that God's call is to be obeyed in every walk of life where 'whether you eat or drink, or whatever you do, do all to the glory of God' (1 Cor. 10: 31).

[26, 34]

7 **CATHOLIC** (Catholicity, Catholicism): In secular use, this word, from the Greek *kath holon* ('by wholeness') indicates breadth of interest or sympathy. Similarly the N.T. 'Catholic Epistles' are those which carry no specific address.

Popularly the term is often simply applied to Roman Catholics (cf. 'Catholic Emancipation'). Though this restriction of the term is resisted by all who confess 'one holy, Catholic Church' in the Creed, another common usage was employed at the Amsterdam Assembly of the World Council of Churches (1948) to contrast Catholic and Protestant. Here the word was assumed to designate those who stress certain features of the Church such as 'visible continuity . . . in the apostolic succession of the episcopate'. This gives to a term which properly belongs to the whole Church a partisan connotation, which should merit the criticism of F. D. Maurice a century ago, who pilloried the words 'Catholic Party'!

It is not a N.T. word, but there we find the universal quality of the Gospel which gathers people of every kind into the Church (Acts 15: 11; Gal. 3: 28, etc.). The actual word is used by Ignatius ('Where Jesus Christ is, there is the Catholic Church') and other early writers, to denote the Universal Church, even in local manifestations, with a Gospel adequate for all men. Later, Cyril of Jerusalem described the Church's catholicity by its being found everywhere, with a complete gospel, for every kind of person, adequate for every moral need.

From this, Catholic implied a claim to be the true as against the false: heresies were localized, not universal, and schismatics were severed from the universal body. So, repudiating these, the Emperor Theodosius spoke of the Catholic Faith, and this was elaborated in the Athanasian Creed as to be believed on pain of eternal damnation. Despite the great Schism of 1054, the West saw a progressive claim to test catholicity by conformity with Rome, and certain Churches of the sixteenth-century Reformation, claiming the word evangelical, replaced catholic in the Creeds by the word Christian. This mainly German development underlies the polarization of terms noted at Amsterdam.

Calvin, on the other hand, wrote:

> . . . the Church is called Catholic or universal, for two or three cannot be invented, without dividing Christ.

Similarly, the *Scots Confession* (1560) speaks of

> one company . . . of men chosen of God who rightly worship and embrace him by true faith in Christ Jesus, who is the only head of the same Church . . . which Church is catholic, that is, universal.

In keeping with this, the Church of Scotland begins its Articles Declaratory of 1922 with the claim to be 'part of the Holy Catholic or Universal Church' and in its baptismal service announces the admission of the baptized to 'the holy Catholic Church'.

The identification of the term with either the Roman obedience or a particular Churchmanship is thus to be treated with reserve. The work of twentieth-century theologians, of many schools, is likely to query the exclusion of any Christian body from the Catholic Church on grounds other than disloyalty to the Gospel itself.

[17, 25]

8 **CELEBRANT** (Celebration): The person who presides when Holy Communion (the Eucharist) is observed (a celebration).

The N.T. gives no ruling on who this shall be, though it may have been those appointed Elders or Bishops. Paul celebrated at Troas (Acts 20: 7-11) but his attitude to Baptism (1 Cor. 1: 17) makes it doubtful if he would have regarded this as essential. On the other hand, his instructions to the Corinthians emphasize the fact that the Lord's Supper is no private meal (1 Cor. 11:20ff) and churches, alert on this point were probably careful as to who should preside. By the end of the century, Clement of Rome stresses respect for those who 'offer the gifts' (1 Clem. 44: 4) to maintain Church unity, and, soon after, Ignatius writes: 'Let that be a valid Eucharist which is celebrated either by the bishop or by someone he authorizes' (*Smyr* 8: 1). From this develops a general concern that the appropriately ordained alone should always be the celebrants.

Clement's words began the process of citing O.T. passages which restrict the offering of sacrifice to priests, under pain of divine displeasure, to support insistence on the prerogatives of Christian ministers (1 Clem. 40–44). The tendency was reinforced when the Eucharist was interpreted in line with Cyprian's words: 'the priest imitates what Christ did'. Then the doctrine of transubstantiation diminished congregational participation in favour of what was believed to be done by the celebrant, even though it might be in private, or as a spectacle. Today, while Roman priests still celebrate daily, even if with only a server, recent Encyclicals and Vatican II emphasize that nevertheless 'no Mass is a private thing' and give preference to celebrations in which others communicate (Encyclical *Mysterium Fidei*, 1965).

Churches are agreed that the celebrant should be one duly authorized, normally by ordination. Certain Churches (e.g. Baptists) hold that the priesthood of all believers implies that in principle any Church member may be the celebrant. Nevertheless, here also normally the one who presides has been set apart by ordination, and even when an unordained person acts, it is not by his own arbitrary decision, but by request and authority of the Church.

Disagreements about ordination itself can lead to differences as to whether or not a celebration is indeed that of the Catholic Eucharist. This arises with certain views of Apostolic succession. On the other hand, the Reformed Tradition, emphasizing the Ministry of the Word, holds that the proper celebrant of either Baptism or the Lord's Supper is the ordained Minister of the Word.

The question of the moral 'worthiness' of the celebrant has also exercised Christians. The Donatists of the fourth and fifth centuries were one of a series of groups who have denied the validity of Sacraments presided over by morally unworthy ministers. None would minimize the duty of ministers to 'walk worthy of their calling'. Yet, knowing that no man is without sin, nor any able to judge another, and that the true Celebrant is Christ Himself, the Church as a whole has not accepted this position.

[11, 31, 34, 39]

9 **CHARACTER:** This Greek noun, cognate with a verb meaning to cut or engrave, implies a distinctive mark or permanent feature, impressed on coin, seal or other object, to make it unmistakably recognizable. It is also applied to a person, and in English is used for the letters of an alphabet, the quality of a language, face or people, and particularly of permanent moral features which make a person what he is. Some idea of stability is always there, and where this is strongly marked a person may even be called 'a character'. If a 'bad character' is notoriously unreliable, this in itself is a permanent feature in his make-up.

Biblically the word is found in Heb. 1: 3 where Jesus is said to carry the character of God's own substance ('the stamp of God's very being' N.E.B.) and is close to the idea of the divine Image in which man was made (Jas. 3: 9) and which is perfectly seen in the Lord Himself (2 Cor. 4: 4). Clement of Rome uses the word in this sense, and Ignatius, on the radical difference between believers and unbelievers, writes:

one might say, surely there are two coinages, one God's, the other the world's. Each bears its own stamp (character) – unbelievers that of this world, believers . . . the stamp of God the Father through Jesus Christ. (Mag. 5.)

These writers seem to be developing the biblical concept of believers as carrying the seal of belonging to God (Ezek. 9: 4–6; Rev. 7: 3f.). This is, in the N.T., most closely associated with the

14

gift of the Spirit (2 Cor. 1: 22; Eph. 1: 13, etc.). This in turn is associated with Baptism (Acts 10: 47; 1 Cor. 6: 11; John 3: 5), which fulfils the function of circumcision as a seal of belonging under the Old Covenant (Col. 2: 11f).

That Baptism is 'once for all' became the settled teaching of the Church ('one baptism for the remission of sins' – Nicene Creed), and from the time of Augustine the term character is used to denote the spiritual quality believed to be indelibly impressed on the soul through Baptism, which compels this view. A developing doctrine of Confirmation as a distinct Sacrament of the gift of the Spirit, opens the way for the view that a further distinct character is impressed through it. This, however, can only be if it is conferred by the proper minister, and he, on his part, was believed to have received a distinct character by ordination. Such teaching concerning Baptism, Confirmation and Ordination, was developed by Thomas Aquinas and was officially endorsed at the Council of Trent. It is held that such distinct characters are so indelibly impressed that even apostasy or expulsion from the priesthood cannot destroy them, and one restored after such a lapse will not be re-baptized or re-ordained.

While the lasting significance of Baptism, Confirmation and Ordination is recognized in most Churches, those of the Reformed tradition have generally been sparing in their use of the metaphor of Character, as leaning towards too mechanistic and deterministic a view of the gifts of grace which must retain a uniquely personal and spiritual quality.

[5, 14, 34]

CHURCH: The Scots form 'Kirk' shows the possibility of a derivation from the Greek *Kyriakon* (belonging to the Lord). The Greek *ekklesia* (cf. 'ecclesiastical'), however, common to the N.T. and the Greek O.T. (where it is usually rendered 'congregation' or 'assembly') implies a body called out and so given an identity. The *ekklesia* of God is the people responsive to the divine calling received by the Christian in Christ.

The word Church is used in various senses:

1. The Universal Church of the Creeds embraces 'the whole Church in heaven and on earth', including the 'company of heaven' (The Church Triumphant) and the whole people of God on earth (The Church Militant).

2. The Visible Church is that people on earth whose story is the material of 'Church history'. Stephen spoke of the 'church in the wilderness' linking the N.T. body with the people of the Old Covenant, whose story began with Abraham. Membership is commonly defined by Baptism, and it is generally understood that the full Christian life involves participation in a visible fellowship. This conviction found sharp expression in Cyprian's phrase, 'outside the Church there is no salvation'. However, one use of the term, the Invisible Church, traceable to Augustine and affirmed at the Reformation, acknowledges that only 'the Lord knows them that are His'. Better established is the Orthodox use of the Invisible Church for the Church Triumphant.

3. A local Church is formed in a particular place by those who unite for common worship and service. The Congregational tradition particularly stresses this usage, which is very common in the N.T., including 'the Church' in a home (Philem. 2). The 'parish church' however also involves this sense of locality, and today there are experiments for forming 'the Church' in a factory or office, where men work, or in a 'house Church' among neighbours.

4. The cohesion of Churches in a defined area is expressed by geographical titles like 'The Church of England', 'The Church of South India', though unwillingness to identify them simply with the area is reflected by a name like 'The Church of Christ in China'.

5. Division for doctrinal, rather than geographical, reasons is commonly called Schism, resulting in distinct denominations, which may even be called Communions, and are also called Churches, e.g. The Roman Catholic Church, the Methodist Church, etc. Some of these, believing themselves to be alone true to essential principles, have withheld the title Church from others, believing Schism to be from the Church. Today this is less common, implying that it may be within the Church, though recognizing this to be contrary to N.T. principles.

6. An old, popular use of the term identifies the Church with ordained ministers or the hierarchy, so that 'to go into the Church' meant to seek ordination. New emphasis on the laity is correcting this practice.

7. The place of worship is often called the church, though the term 'house church' is a reminder that the word properly refers to the people rather than the building in which they meet.

COMMUNION (Eucharist, Lord's Supper, Intercommunion): This word for intimate fellowship, when qualified by the adjective Holy, is a common name for the Sacrament of bread and wine, generally central in Christian worship from apostolic times. Its other names, the Lord's Supper and Eucharist, express respectively its dominical origin and its note of thanksgiving. Holy Communion expresses the fellowship of worshippers with their Lord and consequently with one another:

> The cup of blessing ... is it not the communion of the blood of Christ? The bread which we break, is it not the communion of the body of Christ? For we being many are one bread and one body: for we all partake of that one bread. (1 Cor. 10: 16f., A.V.)

This is a profound expression of mutual sharing 'in Christ' through the Holy Spirit, for which the same Greek word is also used (1 Cor. 1: 9; 2 Cor. 13: 14), as it is for other manifestations

17

of the fellowship, including caring for the material needs of others (Rom. 15: 26, *al*). Further, since union with Christ is not broken by death (Rom. 8: 35ff) the Christian affirms belief in the Communion of Saints in heaven and earth.

Since such Communion depends on our relations with Christ, its inclusiveness is in the N.T. balanced by a certain exclusiveness. Paul denies that it is possible to share in the Lord's Table and that of idols (1 Cor. 10: 21) and asks 'What communion hath light with darkness?' (2 Cor. 6: 14, A.V.). Writing on Church discipline, he directs that a person guilty of unrepented sin be 'delivered to Satan' (1 Cor. 5: 5), implying expulsion from the Church, which is excommunication.

In early times, common participation in this Sacrament, under a proper minister, was the clear expression of unity in each local church, while acceptance at the Lord's Table of Christians from elsewhere, or their ministers, expressed the wider unity of the Church. Thus, locally and universally, Communion expressed unity. In this context, denial of the Sacrament to a person or group of Christians implied a serious decision that such a person or persons were beyond the realm of grace, and to be excommunicated was to be declared anathema, or accursed.

The complex developments of Church history, involving controversies and divisions both geographical and doctrinal, have raised many questions about the mutual relations of Churches. Autonomous bodies, often regionally separate, which fully recognize one another, are said to be 'in communion' or 'full communion' with one another, and such groups may be called a Communion. Those who practise strict exclusiveness in celebrating the Eucharist are said to have 'closed communion'. Those who, while maintaining an orderly discipline for their own members, find no authority to judge those who are in good standing in their own Churches, and believe it right to welcome any such at the Lord's Table are said to practise 'open communion'. Those which have reached an adequate degree of

18

mutual recognition of members and ministers may enter a relation of 'intercommunion'.

[30, 44, 48]

2 COMMUNITY: The word basically indicates the sharing, or holding in common, of property. It has extended to designate a particular body of people who are bound together in a relation of mutual dependence, or in sharing a common life. Such a body may be local, as a school or college community; wider, like the population of a town; or even as wide as the human race, recognized to be interdependent. In a nominally Christian country, the community in this general sense is the body of society within which the Church has a distinct place. In a pluralist or multi-religious society like India, the word has an exclusive reference to those who adhere to a particular religion, e.g. the Hindu community, but is inclusive as comprising all who, however nominally, so adhere. In this context the Christian community, including adherents of different Christian bodies and those who adhere to none, is distinct from what is meant by the Christian Church.

Historically, the term has been used for a body of persons united in the acceptance of a common rule of life, such as the members of a monastic order whose vows include those of poverty, chastity and obedience. The Dead Sea scrolls have brought to light evidence of the rule of life of the Qumran Community of inter-Testamental times. The community of possessions practised by the first Christians in Jerusalem (Acts 2: 44) has stimulated various experiments in communal living among Christians, notably in Germany and, later, in America, of whom the Moravians are among the best known. While some of these have remained in the main stream of Church life and doctrine, others have consciously repudiated any such loyalty.

In modern times, various communities have been formed in

19

different Churches, intended not to rival but to reinforce the general life of the Church. The Anglican Community of the Resurrection, founded in the late nineteenth century, was one of the first of these. Its members sought to apply the classical religious vows to conditions of life and work in the modern world. Other communities have various rules and express purposes, but all require from their members a committal to some rule, which normally includes at least some financial sharing. The Taizé Community in the Reformed Church of France and the Iona Community in the Church of Scotland are among the best known of these. There is always a possibility of the more specific vows and loyalties of such a community seeming to take precedence over the baptismal and confirmation vows which their members share with all members of the Church. But when this is guarded against, such communities have shown themselves well fitted to serve and strengthen the Church as a whole.

[10, 33]

13 **CONFESSION** (Confessor): This word, meaning a clear avowal, may be used either of the Faith, or of Sin.

1. In the O.T. to 'confess the name of God' is to acknowledge Him. In the N.T. to 'confess Christ' before men is welcomed by the Lord Himself. In the epistles it is part of the way of salvation (Rom. 10: 9). Inspired by the Holy Spirit, to say 'Jesus is Lord' is to make such confession.

Later, such a Confession of Faith (a password or symbol) was required at Baptism. Made before the wider world, it meant taking a public stand, costly in times of persecution. The martyr was one whose Confession led to death, while the confessor was one who took his stand at risk of martyrdom or serious loss.

The precise wording of a Confession became important: (a) to form an outline for teaching, (b) to be recited jointly in worship, (c) to define the Faith in controversy, and (d) to express the unity

20

of different local churches. All this applied to the comparatively short Creeds. However, theological debate, especially at the Reformation, led to more elaborate Confessions both to express agreement and to safeguard positions against unbelief or heresy. Such Confessions became tests of orthodoxy, and candidates for ordination were required to assent to them. Churches with a common Confession – e.g. the Lutheran 'Augsburg Confession' or the Presbyterian 'Westminster Confession' – or closely allied Confessions, form families of Churches each of which may itself be called a Confession. Excessive loyalty to these, to the detriment of relations in the wider Church, is stigmatized as Confessionalism. It is to be noted, however, that Churches of the Reformation regard their Confessions as 'subordinate standards', to be tested by Scripture.

Changes in a living language, and sometimes dramatically changing conditions, call for periodic reformulation of Confessions. A striking example was the adoption of the 'Barmen Declaration' by Christians in Germany in 1934, whose stand led to the name Confessional Church. Currently churches in various parts of the world (East Asia, Australia, U.S.A.) are seeking to find new means of 'confessing the faith today'.

2. Confession of sin has always been seen to be involved in reception of forgiveness. We find it in the O.T. (Ps. 32: 5), in the ministry of the Baptist (Mark 1: 5) and in the apostolic Church (Jas. 5: 16). It is made to God, who alone forgives, but there is a ministry entrusted to the Church where confession 'to one another' (Jas. 5: 16) is enjoined. In public worship, corporate confession has a regular place in the approach to God, leading to prayer for pardon, and the announcement of Absolution.

In the Sacrament of Penance, emphasis shifted from public confession to private confession to the priest. Here the priest under a vow of complete confidence, may be entitled one's confessor. Such confession came to be obligatory, particularly before Communion, and in Orthodox Churches one's first

confession marks the transition to responsible Church membership which, in the Western Church, comes with Confirmation.

In Churches of the Reformation, the hearing of confessions,
in strict confidence, continues as part of the 'cure of souls' but
private confession is not obligatory.

[1, 17, 42, 43]

14 **CONFIRMATION:** in association with Baptism, is part of a
whole process of Christian initiation. In Roman Catholic
teaching it is a Sacrament 'in which the Holy Spirit is
given to those already baptized in order to make them strong
and perfect Christians'. In Orthodox Churches, Chrism, with
similar meaning, is also a Sacrament. Other Churches see it as an
Ordinance and means of grace of apostolic origin and accord
importance to its proper administration. In it, prayer for the
Holy Spirit is accompanied by the laying on of hands, or the
raising of hands over the recipient. Anointing with oil (Chrism)
is included in Roman Catholic practice and made central in
Orthodoxy.

Scripture authority for Confirmation, as distinct from
Baptism, is found in narratives which record laying on of hands
by apostles and reception of the Holy Spirit by persons previously baptized (Acts 8: 15-17; 19: 1-6). Other passages
mention reception of the Spirit alongside Baptism (e.g. 1 Cor.
12: 13).

Whether or not the reasons be that apostles were those who
laid on hands in Acts, in Roman and Anglican Churches the
bishop is the regular minister of Confirmation. This is not found,
however, in Lutheran Episcopal Churches, where the parish
minister confirms. The priest also officiates in Orthodox Churches
but uses oil which has been episcopally consecrated.

In Acts 10: 41-48 Baptism is recorded as following reception
of the Holy Spirit. For this reason some Churches have practised

Confirmation or Chrism prior to Baptism. This is rare, for in the official teaching of most Churches, Baptism marks entry into the Church, and other ordinances must follow.

In Orthodox practice, initiation (including Baptism, Chrism and first Communion) is applied to infants, and for many centuries this was general also in the West. From the sixteenth century, however, Roman practice has usually postponed Confirmation at least till the seventh year, and it is prepared for by instruction in the Faith. Though finding no scriptural authority to treat Confirmation as a distinct Sacrament, Calvin pleaded for the restitution of what he believed to be its primitive form, and both Reformed and Lutheran Churches emphasize the preparation of young people for their reception, in face of the congregation, as communicant members of the Church. At this stage, the catechumen makes profession of his faith, accepting the vows made for him at Baptism, and prayer is made for his strengthening or confirmation by the Holy Spirit in the Faith.

Between Churches with such a practice and those which postpone Baptism till a personal confession of faith takes place, there is common ground in the recognition of the appropriateness of Church acts both in infancy – when Baptists have a service of 'dedication' – and when there is personal commitment, signalized by Confirmation. For those baptized in maturity, Confirmation and admission to Communion may take place at one time.

[4, 5, 11]

CONGREGATION (Congregationalism): The word, which in origin denotes the coming together of a company, is extensively used in English versions of the O.T. for the Children of Israel, both when actually assembled in the wilderness (Exod. 16: 10) or at worship (Ps. 22: 22) and as the whole people (Num. 1: 2). (In the N.T. the corresponding Greek word (*ekklesia*) is rendered Church.) In common usage, congregation denotes that body of Church members who habitually meet in a particular locality for Christian worship and joint activities.

In sixteenth-century Scotland, the term The Congregation of the Lord was favoured for the Reformed Church as a whole, and the nobles who played a large part in furthering its interests in their own way were known as The Lords of the Congregation.

Congregationalism appeared in England at the end of the sixteenth century, under the leadership of one Robert Browne. Certain Christians, in their study of the N.T., failed to find any justification for a regional Church. The Church, the mystical body of Christ (Eph. 1: 22f) is known in its membership only to God and so is invisible. The visible Church, on the other hand, is seen only in local bodies (cf. 'the church at Corinth' (1 Cor. 1: 2)). It was therefore held that the proper expression of the Church, and of Church government, is a local congregation or association of believers with their children, bound together 'by a willing covenant made with their God' and so with one another. To such a visible church, dependent directly on Christ as its Head, belongs authority to confess the faith, to worship God, to ordain ministers and to exercise discipline. This polity was widely followed both in England and, soon afterwards, in New England and is practised in various other denominations (e.g. Baptists). Its strength has lain in its recognition of the local church meeting as the authority, that of the whole body, in Church administration (Matt. 18: 17, 20; 1 Cor. 5:3–5). In practice, associations of such Churches, though strictly voluntary, have tended to adopt a stable structure as 'Unions' and have developed even to the point of accepting a regional name as The Congregational Church (in England). Such development in mutual dependence has made it possible for Congregationalists to unite with churches of Presbyterian order (cf. The Church of Christ in U.S.A.) or, along with these, with churches of episcopal order (cf. The Church of South India).

24

In Roman Catholicism, congregations are certain religious societies organized like an order, and bound by vows simpler than those of the regular communities. Also, since the Council of Trent, the Roman Congregations are formally organized departments of the papal *curia*, consisting mainly of Cardinals and presided over each by a Cardinal Prefect, to deal with various ecclesiastical affairs. The 'Holy Office' for faith and morals may be the best known of these.

[4, 12, 19]

COUNCIL (Conciliar): An authoritative body empowered to take corporate decisions on matters of public importance, which may be permanent (cf. The Privy Council) or constituted for a particular occasion (cf. A Council of War).

Councils, convened in particular circumstances, have played a large part in Church History. The council of apostles and elders (Acts 15) met to determine issues from the Gentile Mission. The terms of their verdict 'it seemed good to the Holy Spirit and to us' (v. 28) reflect a confidence in divine guidance which has played a key role throughout. When, from the fourth century, Emperors summoned councils, it was in the declared belief that 'whatever is determined in the holy assemblies of the bishops is to be regarded as showing the will of God'.

In his own area, a bishop might take counsel with his presbyters. Provincial Councils represented a number of Dioceses, and ideally a General Council the whole Church. In these the bishops, as custodians of faith and morals, alone could vote, but advisers were present.

When Constantine I called a General Council at Nicaea (A.D. 325) the concept of an ecumenical Council emerged. Such merit the title not only by their composition, but by the general acceptance of their findings, so that, for example, the Council of Constantinople (381) is reckoned ecumenical. The Western

C

and major Eastern Churches accord this status to seven such Councils (to Nicaea II, 787). However, substantial bodies of Christians, declared heretical (Nestorian and Monophysite) by the Councils of Ephesus (431) and Chalcedon (451) respectively, have not recognized the authority of these, and later, Councils. With them, therefore, a search for agreement must go back earlier, particularly to Scripture.

After 451, and still more after the Schism of 1054, no truly ecumenical council could be held, although some called by the Pope (notably the Lateran Councils of the twelfth and thirteenth centuries) claimed universality. A period of confusion in the Western Church, its chief manifestation being rival Popes (1378–1417) led some to argue that a General Council alone could regulate the Papacy. This 'Conciliar Movement' led to the calling of certain Councils, of which that at Constance (1415–1417) did end the papal schism, but did not establish the theoretical authority of Council over Pope. Yet, when Luther's appeal 'from the Pope ill-informed to the Pope better informed' failed, he turned to the verdict of 'a future General Council of the Church'. Rome has since called the Council of Trent (1547–1560), Vatican I (1870) and Vatican II (1963–1965). The first two of these did much to consolidate papal claims, but Vatican II was concerned with a fresh study of the joint responsibility of bishops.

Reformation documents, in guarded reference to Councils, deny that they are infallible, and exclude any papal claim to control them. In the Reformed tradition, a conciliar polity with a hierarchy of 'courts' from parish to national level was, however, developed (Presbyterianism).

Today the word is used for Christian organizations for joint work. The World Council of Churches co-ordinates a series of regional and national Councils of Churches. These retain an advisory character, but illustrate the basic idea of 'taking counsel together' in the Church.

[22, 38]

CREED: Hard though it is to capture in words the essence of a living faith, Christians have always believed themselves to share a faith 'once for all delivered to the saints' (Jude 3) which one may 'confess with the lips' (Rom. 10: 9). A Creed (Lat. *credo*, I believe) is a declaration of that faith, which may be elaborated for reasons stated in the article 'Confession'.

The word Creed is usually reserved for certain short, pregnant Confessions, more generally acceptable than in one particular tradition. Three such Creeds are commonly called ecumenical, of which the Nicene and the Apostles' have the stronger claim to the title.

(*a*) The Nicene Creed derives its name from the Council of Nicaea (325) where it was largely framed, its main clauses being hammered out to safeguard certain doctrines. Its final form was agreed at the Council of Constantinople (381) and it was re-affirmed on later occasions. Its sections cover Faith in God, Father, Son and Holy Spirit, that on the Son being most elaborated.

(*b*) The Apostles' Creed is shorter but similar in form. Less is known about the later process by which it reached its final wording. Its origin, however, from an earlier Old Roman Creed, can be traced back so far into the early second century as largely to justify the name, though not actual authorship by the apostles.

(*c*) The Athanasian Creed, later and originally in Latin, is more Western, and is an elaborate attempt to formulate what had been accepted as the Catholic Faith regarding the Trinity and the Incarnation.

Having high authority from being framed with general consent in the days of 'the undivided Church', the Creeds, nevertheless, are not an independent source of doctrine, but seek to state correctly what is attested by Scripture. Their recital has a regular place in many liturgies.

In the Reformation Churches they were generally accepted

27

as sound summaries of the Faith, and in the Reformed Church in Scotland, 'the Belief' had an honoured place. However, anxiety to avoid what could become mere repetitions has, in these Churches, checked their regular use in worship, without implying their rejection or debarring their occasional use. Certain Christian bodies, however, stressing liberty of conscience, do not ask their members to subscribe to them.

In some other ways, their universality is incomplete. The Western Church alone added to the confession that the Holy Spirit 'proceeds from the Father' the Latin word *filioque* ('and the Son'). Certain Lutheran Churches, influenced by the partisan use of the word Catholic, substituted the word 'Christian' for it in the Creed. American Methodism, unable to find an acceptable meaning for 'he descended into hell' deleted it. Such modifications would often be necessary if the wording were to be adjusted at each stage to particular understandings; but, while the words remain, it is often found that Christians grow into a new insight into their meaning, and their universality expresses a common, historic faith.

[4, 13, 22, 30]

18 **DEACON** (Diaconate; Deaconess): In Episcopal Churches, a deacon (from the Greek *diakonos*, a servant; cf. *diakonia*, service) belongs to the first order of the ministry, with functions which do not include celebration of the Eucharist. In other Churches it is a lay office concerned with Church administration and service of the needy.

N.T. references to *diakonia* are frequent, regarding both Christ and His Church. He who had come not to be served but to serve, called on His followers to follow the same rule (Mark 10: 43, 45).

In the N.T. Church, forms of service differ with diverse

28

spiritual gifts. An apostle is a *diakonos* as he brings men to the faith (1 Cor. 3: 5) and his distinctive role is his *diakonia* (Acts 6: 4). For others, it is practical service: famine relief to Jerusalem (Acts 11: 29), personal service to St. Paul (2 Tim. 4: 11), or care for widows, for which men of spiritual stature are set apart (Acts 6: 3).

To denote a distinct ministry, the word occurs in Phil. 1: 1, where 'bishops and deacons' are the responsible leaders in the Church, and in 1 Tim. 3: 1–13, where their respective qualities are stated. This technical use of the term soon established itself, writers from Clement onwards speaking of deacons who, alongside bishops, have a distinctive role in worship and in administering alms. In the evolution of this office, the 'Seven' of Acts 6 were taken as the prototype.

Third century and later directions for their ordination and work, stress both the deacon's function and his subordination in a hierarchy. In the East, the diaconate, frequently of a permanent character, became identified more with a distinct function in the liturgy than with wider service. In the Western Church a similar emphasis accompanied a tendency to make it a first stage towards the priesthood.

In Lutheran Churches the diaconate may be separated from the Ministry of Word and Sacrament as a lay vocation for practical service. Congregational and Baptist Churches have seen the deacon's role in Church government complementing the Ministry of the Word. Plans of Church union generally retain the office, but leave the way open for fresh developments.

Probably the earliest N.T. use of *diakonos* for one with a distinct function is in Rom. 16: 1, for a woman, Phoebe, who is commended for her helpfulness to many. This, with Paul's many other appreciative references to the ministry of women (Rom. 16: 3, 6, 13, 15, etc.) including mention of men and women as his 'fellow workers' (Phil. 4: 2f), is a fruit of the Lord's acceptance of the ministry of women, who were the first witnesses of

29

the Resurrection (Luke 24: 22f). Paul's insight was that in Christ is 'neither male nor female'. The revolutionary effect of this development was seen in a fruitful ministry of women, particularly of deaconesses who served the sick and needy and strengthened women catechumens. Later, this ministry led to special orders, and a ministry of compassion marked in various Reformed Churches. Limitations based on two N.T. passages (1 Cor. 14: 33–36; 1 Tim. 2: 9–15) are today not so widely accepted as debarring women from full ordination.

[31, 33, 34]

19 **DISCIPLINE**: In the N.T., discipline, meaning orderliness, is a mark of the Christian life. So far from being opposed to spiritual liberty, as temperance or self-control it is a fruit of the Spirit (Gal. 5: 23). Christ's parable of the pearl of great price, and His call to take up the cross, point to the need for costly choice in responding to Him, and Paul finds it necessary to 'pommel his body and subdue it' (1 Cor. 9: 27).

Orderliness is also expected in the Church, for 'God is not a God of confusion but of peace' (1 Cor. 14: 33) and the Church must exercise discipline to preserve its integrity against moral corruption which, if tolerated, will infect the whole (1 Cor. 5: 6f) and against false teaching which would undermine the truth it exists to proclaim (Gal. 1: 6ff).

Besides this need to guard the Church itself, there is a responsibility to the members. Here authority is found in Christ's words on 'the keys of the kingdom' (Matt. 16: 19) directing that an erring brother be dealt with by the Church which, in the last resort, must expel the recalcitrant (Matt. 18: 17f). Acts and the Epistles have many instances of such discipline which does not overlook the pastoral object of winning the person to repentance by opening his eyes to his condition (cf. 2 Thess. 3: 14f).

The early Church exercised discipline, using as sanctions

30

admonition, suspension from Communion and, in extreme cases, excommunication, with the solemn verdict 'Let him be Anathema'. Developing practices of penance but with no weapons save moral and spiritual authority, its strength was illustrated by such a notable instance as that in which Ambrose of Milan closed his cathedral to the Emperor Theodosius till he atoned for a massacre in Thessalonica.

During this period, however, the Church came to rely on State power to buttress its authority with physical sanctions, a policy upheld by Augustine's use of the text, 'compel them to come in'. This opened the way to a period in which Church discipline was stained by events like a Crusade to crush heretics, and the methods of the Inquisition.

The Reformation did not end alliance with the State, but did bring a new understanding of 'the power of the keys' being exercised in the Ministry of the Word. In Churches relying on Calvin's teaching, Church discipline was held to be a third 'Mark of the Church' with the preaching of the Word and the administration of the Sacraments noted by others. Church polity was set out in *Books of Discipline* (e.g. in Scotland, 1560 and 1578) and this use of the word to cover rules of procedure is still found, e.g. in the Methodist 'Discipline' (U.S.A.). At the same time, Geneva set a pattern of strict supervision of morals of which notable examples were seen in sixteenth-century Scotland and early New England. Discipline has also been exercised in many Churches in trials for heresy and consequent expulsion of ministers and teachers found guilty of false teaching.

Religious communities have their own discipline which may be enforced even physically, once accepted. Besides, the religious life of ordinary Church members may be reinforced by disciplinary rules like fasting on Fridays, or, at one time, strict observance of the Lord's day.

[4, 12, 43, 50]

20 **DISPENSATION:** This word is used in the A.V. both in the sense of the responsible function committed to the apostle, quite apart from his own choice (1 Cor. 9: 17) and for the great Plan of God for Salvation in Christ, of which he is a minister (Eph. 3: 9). Thus it has acquired the technical, theological sense which the corresponding Greek word (*oikonomia*) used in these passages, acquired in early Christian writings. Interpreting various N.T. passages which see in the Incarnation and the Atoning Work of Christ the fulfilment of a great divine Plan, writers like Ignatius, Irenaeus and others, use the word almost as a synonym for Christ's Coming. The Church lives in the time of this Dispensation of Grace, which is also the time in which the saving power of God may be accepted through faith. In the N.T. a contrast is drawn between the attitude of faith and the idle speculation of curiosity seekers (1 Tim. 1: 4).

From this understanding of the Dispensation of Grace in Christ, earlier stages in the unfolding of the divine Plan came to be called Dispensations too. These are the Patriarchal, prior to the work of Moses, and the Mosaic which is dominated by the Law. In keeping with this usage, the R.S.V. finds it appropriate to use the word Dispensation in rendering 2 Cor. 3: 7ff where the Apostle contrasts the situation of the Church with an earlier Dispensation of Death.

In popular, pious parlance, one may speak of Dispensations of 'Providence' or of God Himself to denote circumstances in which we are placed, or the concatenation of events which affect our lives. Those who are less inclined to commit themselves to a religious interpretation of such things may describe them as Dispensations of Nature, though the overtone of a purpose still sounds through the word.

The term is sometimes used in the Church for the Dispensation, meaning the administration, of the Sacraments, and rules governing this will indicate the extent to which it is understood to be a function of the ordained ministry. Such rules can affect the relation between Churches.

Finally, the word is used for the exercise by ecclesiastical authorities of power to release a person, temporarily or permanently, from observance of a particular rule, e.g. that of fasting during Lent. Here again, the authority is likely to be limited to a particular order of the ministry. In Roman Catholic practice, where such rules are fairly common, certain Dispensations can emanate only from the Pope, though others are within the jurisdiction of the bishops.

[3, 21, 26, 31]

ECONOMY: The Greek word *oikonomia*, from which this is derived, is common in the N.T., and in the English Bible is usually rendered by words like stewardship or dispensation. Originally concerned with the management of a household, theologically it denotes first the Plan of God – the divine Economy of grace in Creation and Redemption – which is known through the Gospel (Eph. 1: 10), and then the commission, or stewardship from God, which is given particularly to the Apostles (1 Cor. 9: 17; Eph. 3: 2), for, as authorized witnesses to the Gospel, they are the stewards of the mysteries of God (1 Cor. 4: 1).

This leads to the understanding that the Church is the steward, and its discharge of this commission, particularly in administering the Sacraments is what, especially in the Eastern Church, is basically meant by Economy. In patristic writings the word may refer either to the total administration of the Church, or to particular decisions: e.g. to make provision for a bishop, exiled from his diocese, to continue to exercise his functions.

In Orthodox Churches, the word has become a technical term for administrative action to meet a particular situation, without

33

prejudice to any principle of Church order. While there does not appear to be an official, or authoritative doctrine of Economy, it generally concerns a Church's discretion in matters not covered by binding ecumenical canons. Also, its application basically implies that the Orthodox Churches alone form the true Church, and therefore are the stewards of the mysteries. For this reason, decisions based on Economy appear to be always of a particular nature and to refer to individuals, in their relation to the Orthodox Church, rather than to express a general opinion on the administration of any other Christian body as such.

Such decisions have usually arisen regarding the Sacrament of Baptism or recognition of Ordination. So far as the first is concerned the Orthodox frequently baptize any Christian who enters their fold, on the ground of uncertainty whether his original Baptism was properly trinitarian. In principle, however, they have generally recognized Baptism by others as valid, while teaching that for it to bear fruit (find efficacy), the person concerned should be received into the Church by Chrism. As regards ordination, a similar attitude has been adopted where the Church is satisfied that the proper matter and form have been used, in episcopal ordinations, though here again the rite only becomes efficacious by reception with the laying on of hands.

Participation by the Orthodox in the Ecumenical Movement has been accompanied by a growing willingness to recognize that the free grace of God, and so the working of the Holy Spirit, cannot be limited by the bounds of the Orthodox Church itself. This raises the question of whether an act of Economy gives efficacy to what is already valid or whether it is the other way round. The theory involved depends on the doctrine of the bounds of the Church, as the realm of grace.

[20, 26, 49]

ECUMENICAL (Ecumenism): The word, derived from the Greek *oikoumene* ('the whole inhabited earth', cf. *oikos*, a home) and till recently usually spelt oecumenical, points to the universal character of the Gospel: 'God so loved the world'.

In the early Church, it was used when, by the Roman Peace, it was possible to gather a synod or council from all over the known world. Seven such Councils (to A.D. 787) are generally called Ecumenical, and the faith formulated in them is contained in the Ecumenical Creeds.

Since the Schism of 1054, Eastern (Orthodox) Churches, in full communion with one another, each with its own Patriarch, recognize the Patriarch of Constantinople as 'The Ecumenical Patriarch' – *primus inter pares*. Rome, however, holding that obedience to the Pope is essential to the Church, still claims authority to call a Universal Council, and Vatican II (1964) was summoned as an Ecumenical Synod.

The twentieth century has seen the growth of an 'Ecumenical Movement', named as such by Vatican II, and called 'the great new fact of our time' by Archbishop William Temple. Its roots are many, but a World Missionary Conference at Edinburgh in 1910 played a decisive part. Christian bodies, engaged in Missions, found themselves increasingly drawn into mutual consultation and co-operation, and a permanent International Missionary Council (I.M.C.) with regional Councils, was formed for this. Next, the aftermath of World War I, with problems of human need, awakened Christians to co-operation in service, leading to a Life and Work Movement. Such co-operation, also in student circles, in Y.M.C.A., Y.W.C.A., etc., drove thoughtful Christians to examine their differences and seek the basis of their unity in a Faith and Order Movement. The amalgamation of the second and third of these to form the World Council of Churches (W.C.C.) in 1948, and its union with the I.M.C. in 1961, marked landmarks in the Ecumenical Movement, which is also seen in much local co-operation and work for Church Union in various places. The Greek Orthodox Church, and now also the Russian, are sharers in the work, and there is increasing co-operation with Roman Catholicism, which is now (1968) represented on the Faith and Order Commission.

Ecumenism is a term for activity concerned with such matters. It is when it seems to lead to preoccupation with organizational matters, or to the imposition of a uniform Church structure, that it is criticized as being opposed to the Evangelical. The opposition, however, is superficial and may be resolved.

The Councils down to A.D. 787 were not fully ecumenical, since at least from the early fifth century considerable bodies of Christians, resident mostly outside Roman rule, neither shared in nor accepted the findings of the three or four later Councils. The modern Ecumenical Movement having won the co-opera-tion of these bodies (now commonly called Oriental Orthodox Churches) may in this respect claim to be more comprehensive than at any earlier period. Also, concern for the relevance of the Gospel to man's daily life marks a new emphasis on the word in its basic sense: the whole inhabited earth, man's home.

[10, 17, 46]

23 **ELDER:** In Presbyterian Churches, the title of those appointed to share with the minister in church administration.

Minister and elders form the governing 'court' (or Session) of a local church, responsible to higher courts also consisting of ministers and representative elders. Individually, each elder has a sphere of pastoral responsibility; corporately they have spiritual oversight of the church and its discipline.

The office, and use of the term, are traced back to the O.T., in which elders, heads of leading families, had administrative and legal responsibilities. The institution continued till N.T. times, where the Jewish elders are often mentioned.

36

This precedent was apparently followed when Paul and Barnabas appointed elders in Churches (Acts 14: 23). The appointment of the 'seven' at Jerusalem may have been the choice of elders there. At least, their presence is later taken for granted, when famine relief is entrusted to them (Acts 11: 30) and they share in council with the apostles (Acts 15: 6, 22). General pastoral oversight by elders is implied in Paul's recorded address to those from Ephesus (Acts 20: 28) as in Peter's exhortation as a fellow-elder (1 Pet. 5: 1–4). It may be noted, however, that a somewhat higher authority seems to be claimed when the author of the Johannine letters styles himself simply The Elder (2 John 1; 3 John 1). The title reappears in the mention of four and twenty elders in the visions of Revelation.

In the N.T. with few exceptions, the word is used in the plural. In early writings like those of Ignatius, elders (or presbyters) as a group are distinguished from the single 'overseer' or bishop, and in episcopal polity, the term is absorbed in the title presbyter or priest and used for the middle order of the ministry, distinct from the bishop. Certain other bodies (e.g. the Moravians) have, however, retained the title Elder for their senior ministers.

Presbyterian polity, claiming precedents from the early Church, and observing both the O.T. pattern and the inclusion of 'administrators' in Pauline lists of spiritual gifts (1 Cor. 12: 28) has retained the term 'Ruling' Elder for an office distinct from the Ministry of Word and Sacrament. One theory would classify them alongside these, by entitling the latter 'preaching' or 'teaching' Elders, in reliance on texts like 1 Tim. 5: 17 which speaks of preachers who also 'rule well'. On this theory the ordination of Elders is parallel to that of ministers and theirs ceases to be a lay office. This interpretation is not found in a classical document like the *Westminster Confession* nor in the *First Book of Discipline* (1560) which provided for their annual election. Practice today varies, some Churches 'ordaining' for life to what is recognized as a lay office, others providing for term as well as life Elders. Common to all is a high valuation of this ministry by persons engaged in ordinary secular avocations. Once a male preserve, the eldership is now in many cases open to women.

[31, 33, 34]

24 **EPISCOPACY** (Bishop; Episcopate; *Episkopé*): The word reflects the underlying concept of superintendence (Greek *episkopé*) as an essential element in the Church's ministry. While the word *episkopé* is rare in the N.T. the concept recalls Christ's commission to Peter (John 21: 15–17) and the charge to the Ephesian elders to care for the flock 'in which the Holy Spirit has made you *episkopoi*' (Acts 20: 28). Episcopacy, then, is that Church polity which recognizes different orders in the ordained ministry, and sees the bishops as the highest of these, the chief pastors of the flock. Each bishop is responsible in a defined territory (diocese) for functions which include the ordination and authorization of other ministers, supervision of worship including the Sacraments, and safeguarding doctrine. He is generally the minister of Confirmation. In a wider territory, the bishops, presided over by one of their number – archbishop, primus or metropolitan – from a corporate Episcopate responsible for the Church as a whole. In England certain bishops have a seat in the House of Lords.

(Within Roman Catholicism, the supremacy of the Pope has tended to overshadow the bishops, though this may be corrected as an outcome of Vatican II statements on their corporate responsibility. Churches of Presbyterian polity, recognizing full responsibility for each minister in his own charge, provide for corporate *episkopé* to be exercised by them, together with elders, through a hierarchy of Church courts.)

38

Episcopacy can claim ancient history, widespread acceptance, and a flexibility manifested in wide variety. The last ranges from second-century situations – and some 'missionary' situations today – in which a single congregation may have its own bishop, to vast dioceses based on provincial boundaries, in which the bishop becomes a remote and exalted dignitary. The system also has proved capable of being used even without unanimity as to the underlying theory.

The early evolution of episcopacy is obscure, but by the end of the second century there seems to be a universal distinction between the group of presbyters and their single, presiding, bishop. In the third century writers like Cyprian draw out the importance of each bishop in his diocese, and the necessity of orderly succession in office. By the fourth century, the practice whereby each bishop is consecrated by other bishops is apparently universally accepted. This last aspect of succession, especially when associated with the conviction that the office has always been distinct from that of presbyters (corresponding rather to the N.T. apostles), leads to a theory of apostolic succession according to which bishops form the 'essential ministry' on which all others, and so also the Sacraments, are dependent. This theory makes the life of the Church itself depend on the Historic Episcopate, one linked by successive consecrations with the apostles.

There are, however, Churches with an episcopal polity, which regard it as fitting and scripturally justified, without claiming this interpretation. Others value the succession of consecrations as witnessing to the continuity of the Church, but not as essential to its very being. Conclusive evidence to establish a theory is lacking.

[3, 31]

25 **EVANGELICAL** (Evangel, Evangelism, Evangelist): Evangel
is almost a transliteration of the Greek for Gospel, which
means 'good news' of salvation through Jesus Christ.
Evangelism is the sharing of that news, and the evangelist one
who proclaims it. Evangelical is strictly an adjective applied to
things that belong to the Gospel. The belief that the monastic
life, governed by vows of poverty, chastity and obedience,
conforms to the Gospel ideal explains why these are traditionally
known as the Evangelical Counsels.

On the European continent, this adjective (corresponding to
the English Protestant) designates Churches of the Reformation
over against Roman Catholicism. This has led to a classification
of Christians as Evangelical or Catholic, which obscures the
proper meaning of both words.

In the English-speaking world, the term has been used for
Christians of different Churches who are zealous for the Gospel,
understood in terms of a conservative, trinitarian theology. They
have tended to stress individual salvation, and to hold a substitu-
tionary theory of the Atonement, while emphasizing the
plenary inspiration and authority of Scripture. United in such
convictions, evangelicals have been responsible for the foundation of different missionary societies, revival movements and
religious conventions where conversion is emphasized. Some
whole denominations are classified as evangelical in this sense;
in others an Evangelical Party has been identified, as contrasted
with High Churchmen (or Catholics) in England or with the
Moderates of the early nineteenth-century Church of Scotland.

In 1846 a group of like-minded members of various Churches
were led to form an Evangelical Alliance with the avowed aim
of promoting Christian unity and religious tolerance. Taking
the motto 'We are one body in Christ', this Alliance sought to
take seriously our Lord's Prayer for the unity of His people, and
among other things began the universal observance of an annual
week of prayer. Composed of individuals rather than Churches,
40

the Alliance defined its position by formulating articles of faith expressing a biblical, trinitarian, sacramental but non-sacerdotal theology. This basis, which excludes alike Liberal, Unitarian, Quaker and Roman positions, tended to build up an interpretation of the Faith contrasted with that of those who stress the corporate Church with ordered ministry and sacraments.

The twentieth century has seen something of a world-wide polarization of evangelical and ecumenical, the latter being considered to be too concerned with questions of ecclesiastical structure rather than with Evangelism. The missionary roots of the Ecumenical Movement, so largely a fruit of a common concern for the Gospel, are a powerful support for those who claim both adjectives as proper for the Christian Church.

[40, 42]

GRACE (Means of Grace): A word, normally indicating charm or comeliness, means, in Theology, the graciousness or generosity of God making possible what man cannot do for himself. In the preaching of the Gospel, it is especially seen in Christ's saving work, and so may be called Saving Grace. For this reason, in the Christian era we are said to live in years of grace. The Christian believer also recognizes Sustaining Grace in the divine mercy by which all men live and Prevenient Grace in God's hand on the life of one who may only late come to conscious faith. There is also a Sanctifying Grace by which the Christian is enabled to grow to spiritual maturity, and gifts of grace manifest consequent spiritual qualities.

These usages conform to that essentially personal understanding of God's grace stated above. Charged with proclaiming the Gospel and 'feeding the flock of Christ', the Church believes itself to be an instrument used by God in His gracious dealings with His children. While, in His sovereign grace, He

D

may indeed use other means to this end, the Christian from childhood is encouraged to make diligent use of such regular means of grace as the practice of prayer, public worship, the reading and hearing of God's Word, and the Sacraments.

While the above would probably be acceptable in most of the Church, a different understanding is reflected in phrases like 'a state of grace' and its negative 'a fall from grace'. These words imply a condition or quality of life which, by the grace of God, has been given to a person to be in some sense his possession, though it may be marred or lost by sin. This condition is understood to be one to which God has been pleased to raise a person, which is higher than his natural state. The Council of Trent described it as 'an inherent, divinely infused perfection', and spoke of Habitual Grace. The view is accompanied by a strict understanding that it is conveyed by the Church, as a divinely authorized hierarchical body which controls the administration of the means of grace. Thus Vatican II states that 'from the Liturgy, and especially the Eucharist, as from a fountain, grace is channelled to us'.

Such language may obscure the essentially personal character of grace. In medieval times, it was the Church's control of these means which made effective the weapons of excommunication of an individual, or an Interdict on a whole region, withdrawals of the Church's ministrations which were believed to shut up the channels of grace itself. Today a new awareness of the multitudes beyond the sound of the Gospel who have been nurtured in other faiths, also of the common faith in Christ shared by Christians of other traditions, has led to a more serious recognition of the grace of God at work beyond the limits of our organizations, but not beyond Him in whom it is God's will to sum up all things.

[14, 21, 44]

HOLY (Holiness, Saint, Sanctify): In Isaiah's vision, he heard the seraphim, their faces veiled in reverence, cry 'Holy, holy, holy is the Lord of hosts' (Isa. 6: 2). This catches the basic sense of the holiness of One who is ineffable, beyond all mortal telling. In Moses' vision at the burning bush, he was commanded to remove his shoes, for this was holy ground (Exod. 3: 5). Here the adjective is applied to a place (as it may be to an object or time), which is set apart for the presence, or service of God.

These examples illustrate our use of the word, when we speak of God the Holy Spirit, of the book through which He is revealed as the Holy Bible, the country in which sacred history was unfolded as the Holy Land. Holy vessels are set apart for sacramental use, and the Holy Table for the Sacrament. Men are ordained to the Holy Ministry, and the observance of Holy Week leads up to Easter. Always there is a setting apart for God.

The revelation of God as righteous and loving leads the Christian to understand that the holy should also be morally pure, an idea dominant in popular usage. Devotion to Christ and purity of character are implied in recognizing a holy man or woman, which is the meaning of the title Saint, derived from a Latin word of this meaning. This is traditionally applied to particular persons (e.g. the evangelists, St. Augustine) either by popular recognition (e.g. the Celtic saints) or by canonization by Church Authority as became common in the Western Church. Nevertheless, in the N.T. it is all believers who are 'called to be saints' (1 Cor. 1: 2). The fact that in Christ they have been washed and sanctified implies this calling (1 Cor. 6: 11) and should lead to a life worthy of it (Eph. 4: 1). Consequently, in Church history, despite the peril of a reputation for holiness being degraded into one for sanctimoniousness, this calling has been taken in all seriousness, as in *A Serious Call to a Devout and Holy Life* (William Law), or the Holy Club which the young Wesley and his friends formed, or when Christians of different denominations seek to cultivate this quality in Holiness Conventions today.

Holiness is one of the Notes or Marks of the Church indicated in the Creeds (the Holy, Catholic Church). This is because its very being depends on its relation to Christ (1 Cor. 1: 2). Paul means the whole company, not just some outstanding souls, when he speaks of the saints (1 Cor. 6: 2) who form that Church locally, and the Gospel also requires the offering of the whole of life to God's service: 'whether you eat or drink, or whatever you do . . .' (1 Cor. 10: 31). Thus the phrase 'The communion of the Holy Spirit' (2 Cor. 13: 14 A.V.) implies that paradox of the Gospel which claims not some but all, and their common life, for the Holy One. Some awareness of this appears in current concern for the common life of men, which may be called 'secular' but should not be separated from the Faith. The dedication of places, times or objects for sacred use should not obscure the vision of when 'every pot in Jerusalem' is to be sacred to the Lord (Zech. 14: 21).

[6]

28 **INVOCATION** (Epiclesis): An earnest plea for God's presence and blessing. In such a prayer, awareness of the nature of the God thus addressed, is expressed by the use of descriptive terms. When Moses at the burning bush wanted to know God's name (Exod. 3: 13) he probably shared a widespread belief that effective prayer for blessing by a deity depended on ability to use his proper name. While the Bible repudiates the notion that God the Lord can thus be compelled by human means, nevertheless the worshipper calls on Him in terms which show understanding of His distinctive being. Paul, remembering the promise that whoever calls on the name of God will be saved, reminds us that none can call on Him of whom they have not heard (Rom.

44

10: 14). Jesus addressed the Father as 'Lord of heaven and earth' (Matt. 11: 25) and Peter speaks of calling on Him as the Father who judges impartially (1 Pet. 1: 17).

To take the name of God implies the thought of His presence as the august Witness of men's pledges, as when Laban and Jacob pledge loyalty at Mizpah and know that He will watch between them (Gen. 31: 49). Negatively, Jeremiah pictures as desolate a time when men will no longer call on His name, saying 'as the Lord God lives' (Jer. 44: 26). In the Sermon on the Mount, Jesus gives warning against any light use of such expressions (Matt. 5: 33–37).

In Christian worship, not only is the opening prayer, frequently to the Holy Trinity, an Invocation, but so is the short prayer, or acknowledgement: In the name of the Father, and of the Son and of the Holy Spirit, which precedes the sermon. There is an Invocation of God at Baptism, and special prayer for strengthening by the Holy Spirit, with the laying on, or uplifting, of hands, at Confirmation.

In the Liturgy of Holy Communion, ancient and modern, there is traditionally a special Invocation or prayer for the Holy Spirit, which is known as an *Epiclesis* (Greek). This follows the prayer of thanksgiving, which includes a recalling of Christ's actions and also the setting out of the elements to be used. This Epiclesis seeks the blessing of the Holy Spirit on the elements, that they may be the very body and blood of Christ, and on the worshippers. This probably underlies Augustine's saying that when the Word is added to the Element it becomes a Sacrament. St. John Chrysostom on his part is quoted as saying that the priest does not, like Elijah, call down fire from heaven but the Holy Spirit 'that the Grace falling on the sacrifice may through it inflame the souls of all'. Consequently the Eastern Church does not stress a single moment of consecration, but shows a lively sense of the transforming power of the Holy Spirit both in the elements and in the worshipping body. In the West, the doctrine of Transubstantiation brought a belief in an actual change in the elements through repetition of Christ's declaratory words: 'This is my body'. Reformed Churches generally retain an Invocation of the Holy Spirit, to bless the elements and that the worshippers may be enabled 'to feed on Him by faith with thanksgiving'.

[5, 11, 14]

29 **LAYMAN** (Laity): Today this word is often used negatively in fields like medicine, law, etc., to indicate the uninstructed as against the professional. This derives from a Church tradition in which the laity in contrast to 'the clergy' were so regarded. Lay brothers in religious orders are defined largely by what they are not authorized to do. In churches, the congregation occupies the nave, a word meaning the body of the ship where the passengers (laity) are segregated from mariners. In another metaphor they are the flock dependent on their pastors.

This negative understanding has never been wholly accepted. Originally the term is positive. From the Greek *laos* (people) and *laikos* (of the people) the words recall the biblical notion of 'the people of God', and particularly passages which claim for the Church the promised status of 'a chosen race, a royal priesthood, a holy nation, God's own people' (1 Pet. 2: 9). Members are initiated by Baptism and commissioned for service in Confirmation. In this light, Tertullian could say: 'Are not we laics also priests?'

In the N.T., instructions to the body of believers (1 Cor. 5: 4f) and the Council of Jerusalem where apostles and elders assembled with 'the whole church' (Acts 15: 22) show that all shared in decision making. The appointment of the Seven (Acts 6) shows a choice made by the whole people. Descriptions of worship in 1 Cor. 14 suggest a shared leadership and participation by all.

46

While the early centuries show movement towards the rule of bishops, Cyprian insists that they act with the consent of the people, and in the choice of clergy an important part is played by their voice.

Many Churches reserve doctrinal decisions to the ordained, though in Presbyterian practice elders share in all verdicts, and the layman has full place in councils of Congregational polity. In administrative and other matters, however, both local and regional, most Churches, including the Roman of Vatican II, are moving to increased lay participation. An effective voice in selecting ministers has in some areas been reserved to certain lay patrons, and a practice akin to the Reformed 'call by the congregation' is becoming more common. In worship, the authorization of lay readers or licensing of lay preachers recognizes a service to be rendered by many besides ordained ministers.

The Reformed tradition reserves administration of both Gospel Sacraments to the ordained, and expresses 'the priesthood of all believers' by provision for worshippers to share in 'giving and receiving' the elements. By contrast, most Episcopal Churches, quoting early precedent, recognize lay Baptism in emergencies, but do not authorize lay celebration at Holy Communion. Some Baptist and Congregational Churches believe such celebration exhibits a biblically based doctrine of 'the priesthood of all believers'.

Outside such matters, it is today more widely seen that the layman earning his livelihood in the secular world has direct responsibility for Christian life and service there. Other ministries are a gift to equip him for this lay apostolate (cf. Eph. 4: 12).

[15, 33]

LITURGY (Liturgics; Worship): Worship, humble and adoring acknowledgement of the worth of God, is the proper response of man to his Maker ('Man's chief end is to glorify God' – *Shorter Catechism*) and corporately is the primary function of the Church. From N.T. days it has always assembled for worship (Acts 2: 42) and the pattern followed in such common worship is its Liturgy. The term is most commonly applied to the service of Holy Communion, with its successive acts of adoration, thanksgiving, consecration, etc. While it is a term often avoided by Churches which encourage 'free' prayer, nevertheless they also usually follow a regular pattern, with congregational participation in hymns, etc., which is essentially their Liturgy.

The word *leitourgia*, which in classical Greek denoted personal service to the State, was in the Greek O.T. applied to priestly service in the temple. Though infrequent in the N.T. this word, and that for one who performs such service (*leitourgos*), is found. Paul uses it for the actions of Christians who cared for the material needs of others (Rom. 15: 27; 2 Cor. 9: 12) and speaks of his bringing Gentiles to Christ as his own priestly service (Rom. 15: 16).

In sub-apostolic writings the word is used for Christian worship. It implies an orderly pattern for this in which all participants have their appropriate part, and also reflects the understanding that such worship continues that of the O.T. The Liturgy of the Eucharist early took a shape which has largely continued. In this the non-baptized were present for the first part – the Liturgy of the Word – but only communicants at the second, the Breaking of the Bread. Such a Liturgy involved both words and symbolic actions. There also evolved a liturgical year to recall the great events of the Gospel, and even liturgical colours to mark the various seasons of that year. The comparative study of Liturgies and their history is known as Liturgics.

The use of a Liturgy provides for the meaningful participation

48

of all worshippers. Also by following a pattern of worship used in earlier generations, it expresses the continuity of the worshipping Church, and enables each worshipper or local group to enter a heritage much richer than any alone could find. Evidence of such worship in the N.T. (e.g. Rev. 4: 8–11; 5: 9–14) is coupled with the vision of it going on in heaven, so that the prayers of the Church Militant are mingled with those of the Church Triumphant (Rev. 8: 2–5), a concept which is expressed in some of the most exalted language of today's Liturgies, and is especially marked in those of the Orthodox Churches.

Continued use of the Liturgy has, even in times of persecution, preserved the Church's confession of Faith and response to the Gospel. Such worship is, however, criticized, when it leads to the continued use of archaic language, even languages no longer understood (e.g. Syriac or Latin). The twentieth century has seen attempts at Liturgical Reform, both to secure more meaningful participation by all among those which use older Liturgies, and to bring the treasures of the Church's heritage to those which have had a more 'free' tradition.

[11]

MINISTRY (Minister): means service, and the N.T. recognizes particular forms of service as commissioned by God (2 Cor. 4: 1). State authorities are called 'God's ministers' (Rom. 13: 2), dim though the recollection of this may be among modern Ministers of State. Christ came to minister (Mark 10: 45) and His apostles knew that they were charged with a ministry in preaching His Gospel, the ministry of reconciliation (2 Cor. 5: 18).

Besides the apostles' ministry, passages like 1 Cor. 12: 28 list that of many others as the gift of the Holy Spirit. In the Pastoral Epistles directions for appointing bishops or elders and deacons

49

(1 Tim. 3: 1–13, 5: 17; Titus 1: 5ff) show a more stabilized picture. Some have sought to classify such ministries as 'charismatic' (Spirit-inspired) and 'official' (formally appointed), but in the N.T. all ministries are seen as the gift of the Spirit. There is more reason to distinguish a local from an itinerant ministry, a distinction explicit in the *Didache* where exhortations to respect local ministers imply that itinerant 'prophets' enjoyed higher esteem.

Another distinction emerges in the N.T. when the apostles found themselves unduly burdened and asked for men to serve tables, leaving them free to serve the Word (Acts 6: 1–6). This is widely regarded as the first making of deacons, and in Phil. 1: 1 we have bishops and deacons mentioned as distinct groups. In the N.T. elders and bishops are never listed as distinct, and the evidence suggests that they were the same people, elders in standing, bishops (overseers) in function. A distinction emerges clearly in the second century (see Episcopacy).

The Preface to the Anglican Ordinal stresses the fact that the three titles (Bishop, Priest, Deacon) are from earliest days, and we meet the claim that there is historically a 'threefold ministry'. Functions however, have varied greatly and the hierarchy has extended upwards to Metropolitan, Patriarch and Pope, and downwards to sub-deacons and readers. These considerations increase the reserve with which others treat the notion of the threefold Ministry, and the Geneva Reformers recognized one order of ministers of Word and Sacrament, as God's essential gift to the Church, continuing the work of the apostles. Alongside it they recognized the ruling elder, the administrative deacon, and the learned doctor of the Church.

Reformation (including Anglican) documents freely use the title minister for the ordained. The use has diminished in Episcopal Churches, but is elsewhere retained as 'Minister of the Gospel' or 'of the Word of God'. Since, however, the entire Church is called to Ministry, the inclusive term for the ordained is often 'the ordained (or Holy) Ministry'. Other phrases like 'the ministry of the laity' indicate the wider service in which all share.

From earliest years there has been a distinctive ministry of women chiefly as deaconesses. Though the ordained Ministry is now in many Churches also open to women, this distinctive service will not be lost.

[18, 23, 24, 33]

NATURAL (Nature, Spirit, Spiritual): Seen through the eyes of Jesus, the orderly processes of Nature express the benevolent faithfulness of God (Matt. 5: 45). Paul also sees in them the evidence of God's hand, as he sharply reminds the men at Lystra who wish to pay him divine honours (Acts 14: 17). He spoke similarly at Athens (Acts 17: 26) and declared it possible to recognize God's hand in Nature, in a passage on man's failure to do so (Rom. 1: 20). Paul also thinks that 'nature herself' gives us a sense of what is becoming in man and in woman (1 Cor. 11: 14) and argues that men, by nature, can make moral judgements (Rom. 2: 14). From this basis, theologians built up a doctrine of Natural Law and a Natural Theology, teaching that grace completes but does not destroy Nature, and Revealed Theology crowns what is discoverable by reason.

The Greek word here translated Nature is *physis*, but another N.T. word, *psychikos*, often translated natural, implies something seriously deficient. The natural man is blind to spiritual things (1 Cor. 2: 14). James (3: 15) and Jude (19) use the word to connote our sensual nature, devoid of the Spirit. Nor is this just a neutral deficiency: it implies a sinful infection which has corrupted man's nature, an alienation which requires not just completion but healing and reconciliation. The blindness which

51

prevents man from recognizing God in Nature is due to wickedness (Rom. 1: 21). Paul recognizes this alienation in himself, where another law in his members is at war with the law of the mind (Rom. 7: 22). Men have become by nature 'children of wrath' (Eph. 2: 3) and somehow the infection has affected the natural world, so that the whole creation waits with longing for the revealing of the sons of God (Rom. 8: 19). Thus the teaching that grace fulfils nature must be supplemented by the insight that what is needed is not just an addition but a healing.

Against this background, we see the N.T. teaching on the spiritual, created by the mercy of God. Man must be born anew of water and the Spirit (John 3: 5), and those who are led by the Spirit of God are the sons of God (Rom. 8: 14). The spiritual man thus formed alone is in a position to judge all things (1 Cor. 2: 15). Against the tendency to identify the spiritual with the ecstatic, Paul finds the token of His work in witness to Christ (1 Cor. 12: 3; cf. John 16: 14), and in what edifies the Church, the heart of which is love (1 Cor. 13: 13).

A contrast between physical and spiritual is not found in the N.T., but in Gnosticism it led either to extreme asceticism (an attempt to nourish the spirit at the expense of the body) or to libertinism which, claiming freedom from the body, allowed its appetites free reign. This contrast can also oppose Church structure to spiritual unity. The N.T. however has 'one body and one Spirit' (Eph. 4: 4) and life in Christ is building a 'spiritual house' (1 Pet. 2: 5). The N.T. contrasts the natural and the spiritual, the former determined by earthly instincts, the latter by the gift of the Holy Spirit. This makes possible the thought of a 'spiritual body' (1 Cor. 15: 44) and faith in 'the resurrection of the body' rather than 'immortality of the soul'. It also makes possible the Sacraments in which material things are means of grace for spiritual ends.

[26]

ORDER (Orders): To enable a company of people to share in an act of common worship, without the distraction of uncertainty as to what each item will be, it is customary to have an agreed sequence of praise, prayers, readings, etc. This is an Order of Service. When the act is one regularly repeated, public worship, the Sacraments of Baptism, the Lord's Supper, or an Ordination, it is usual for Church authorities to prescribe an Order for such acts. This is often based on an Order of great antiquity. Where the precise words to be used throughout are prescribed, it may be called a fixed Liturgy, but there are gradations from uniformity even in detail to wide freedom in the words used within an agreed Order. Thus the *Book of Common Prayer* in Anglican tradition may be compared with a *Book of Common Order* in Scottish, the latter being a guide and model and not a form to be strictly adhered to.

Information about such Orders of worship are found in early Christian documents and are adumbrated in Scripture, e.g. in Paul's precise outline of the institution of the Lord's Supper (1 Cor. 11: 23–26). Further, the conviction that the freedom of the Spirit in common worship, so far from forbidding order actually requires it, is seen in the call for that considerateness which is marked by speaking 'each in turn' (1 Cor. 14: 27) and the reminder that God is not a God of confusion with the plea that all be done 'decently and in order' (1 Cor. 14: 33, 40).

Orderliness in worship was in the O.T. provided through the institution of the Aaronic priesthood, within which different persons had functions to perform in turn (Luke 1: 8f). This is superseded by the high priestly work of Christ (Heb. 7: 16f) and the N.T. provides no evidence of any new priestly Order, within the priestly people (1 Pet. 2: 5). There is, however, much evidence in the N.T. of the setting apart and recognition of leaders to whom respect is due (Acts 14: 23; Heb. 13: 17, *al*). From such beginnings there emerges in the early Church a more settled pattern of a ministry, where different functions are assigned to different Orders, the most familiar being those of bishops, presbyters and deacons. The solemn act of setting persons apart for such ministry (Ordination) came to be understood as conferring on them a special character, namely that of Holy Orders. Further, in many Churches deaconesses are considered to form another distinct Order of ministry. It must be noted, however, that the theory underlying this was challenged at the Reformation by those who regarded it as an unwarranted return to O.T. concepts.

A further use of the word is related to religious communities, formed on the basis of a particular rule of life, and recognized by competent authority. Admission to such a community is often stated to be into a particular Order, with avowed rules and purposes, such as Benedictines, Franciscans or Dominicans.

[4, 9, 30, 31]

34 **ORDINATION** (Ordinal; Ordinand): Related to ordain and ordinance, words referring to matters determined by high authority, this means the orderly commissioning of a person (the ordinand) for the Holy Ministry. Christ commissioned the apostles (John 20: 22f) and they the Seven (Acts 6: 6) and elders (Acts 14: 23) while Timothy had hands laid on him by Paul and the presbytery (2 Tim. 1: 6; 1 Tim. 4: 14). Each time it is understood that the person received the gift of the Holy Spirit for his work.

Different verbs may be used for this commissioning – the Making of Deacons, the Ordering of Priests, the Consecration of Bishops – but these, and only these, are covered by the term Ordination with laying on of hands. Without that rite, some Presbyterian Churches use the same term for the appointment of Ruling Elders.

An Ordinal is the Order of Service for Ordinations. Many of these are extant from the fourth century onwards. They show the whole Church involved in the act, the people signifying assent, the ordained ministry officiating. Common to them are prayer (invoking the gift of the Spirit and specifying the ministry to which the person is ordained) and Laying on of Hands by ministers possessing the requisite authority: in Episcopal Churches, the bishops, accompanied by presbyters, in Presbyterian the ordained members of the Presbytery, in Congregational Churches, Church representatives and other ministers. Besides these constants, other customs are known, particularly the solemn delivery to the ordinand of instruments to be used in his ministry. In Roman Catholicism these are the paten and chalice, for use in the Mass, while the ordination formula includes: 'Receive power to offer the sacrifice'. In other traditions it is a Bible, implying service of the Word. The Western Church increasingly used imperative or declaratory formulae such as 'Receive the Holy Ghost for the office and work of . . .' This may alter the emphasis from prayer that God will ordain, to an act of the ordaining ministers, opening the way to controversy on the credentials of these ministers, and the consequent validity of the Ordination. There is, however, common ground in humble awareness that any true Ordination must be by God Himself, who uses human instruments.

The Ordinand is properly one called to a particular charge or office. Nevertheless the major Churches agree that it is to a lifelong ministry in the universal Church. (Exceptionally, some churches of 'independent' tradition believe a person's ministry to be bound up with his particular charge.) Such understanding and intention rule out proposals for re-ordination or 'supplementary' ordination to unite divided ministries. The argument that all ministries in separation are defective goes too far. Whether united or separate, they depend on divine grace, which is always divine generosity.

Nothing in Scripture or early history, requires that those ordained to the Holy Ministry must make it their livelihood. Yet this has been so common that Ordination is commonly thought to imply it. Today fresh proposals for 'voluntary' or 'part-time' ministries are seeking to change this.

[26, 33]

35 **ORTHODOX** (Orthodoxy): Derived from the Greek for 'right opinion', Orthodoxy in any field denotes a generally accepted pattern of belief or conduct. It can establish itself in any circle or sect, including those which began as revolutionary, as witness Communist charges of 'Deviationism'!

It is not a Bible word, but the N.T. has passages which underline the importance of 'sound doctrine' (Titus 2: 1). Paul, resisting perverse teachings, protested that there is not 'another gospel' (Gal. 1: 7). The pastoral epistles wish to maintain 'the pattern of sound words' (2 Tim. 1: 13) and see the Church as 'the pillar and bulwark of the truth' (1 Tim. 3: 15). This, as it can be formulated, is in Jude 3 that 'which was once for all delivered to the saints'.

Though 'right opinion' can never adequately express spiritual truth, the Church, challenged by heterogeneous teachings, early found it necessary to seek precise formulation of its belief. Regional Churches made their Confessions, and together they sought agreement in Ecumenical Councils, their various definitions seeking to express what was believed 'always, everywhere and by all' (Vincent of Lerins) (Catholicity).

The evolution of Church history, entangled in the changing fortunes of the Empire, brought strains between other Patriarchs and the Bishop of Rome. Finally, Rome's adoption of a clause (*filioque*) in the Apostles' Creed, without the sanction of an Ecumenical Council, led to the Great Schism of 1054. Thereafter the Greek Churches of the East held to the name Orthodox to signify loyalty to the ancient Faith and refusal of a Roman claim to jurisdiction over other Churches.

Missionary expansion led to Churches of similar outlook being established in the Slavonic world, of which the Russian became the largest. With a high doctrine of the Church, and firm loyalty to their liturgy, these Churches have endured through centuries of adverse external conditions including Moslem and (more recently) Communist domination. They see themselves a federation of autocephalous Churches (each with its own head) confessing the faith witnessed to by the seven Ecumenical Councils. They emphasize the wholeness of the Church, as in the Russian concept of *sobornost* (togetherness) and in worship which stresses this theme: 'Let us love each other in order that we may be worthy to express in union our faith'. Strict in doctrine and claim, the Orthodox have been drawn into common services with others and into a growing share in the World Council of Churches.

The catholicity of these Churches is obscured by their strong national characteristics. However, factors such as emigration to America, the dispersal of Russian believers after the 1917 Revolution, and a new missionary interest, are affecting this aspect. Further, Orthodoxy cannot ignore those bodies which were alienated from the Greek and Latin Churches in the fifth century and which today are located in India, Ethiopia and elsewhere. These hold a firm conviction that, unjustly condemned at Ephesus (431) or Chalcedon (451), they have kept the Faith. Today the Ecumenical Movement has seen steps towards understanding between these Oriental Orthodox (see p. 36) and the Eastern Orthodox Churches.

[7, 13, 22]

36 PARISH (Diocese, Province): The words denote progressively larger units in the territorial arrangements of a settled Church, designed to ensure a regular provision for the Ministry of Word and Sacraments, and for pastoral care, within the whole area of responsibility. Though sometimes adapted to a more obviously missionary situation, basically the system belongs to the concept of Christendom, where citizens are assumed to owe some allegiance to the Church. Parish (*paroikia*) and diocese (*dioikesis*) are from Greek compounds which include the word *oikos*, a house. The first refers to a compact area, usually with one congregation with priest or minister. The Greek word for the second originally referred to housekeeping or administration. It denotes a larger territory, comprising many parishes, under the jurisdiction of one bishop. (In non-episcopal Churches corresponding territories are differently named.) A number of dioceses, linked around a Metropolitan See, form a Province governed by a senior bishop who may be styled Metropolitan, Archbishop, Primus or some other term. Certain religious Orders, e.g. the Jesuits, are also organized by Provinces, the superior being called the Provincial.

The New Delhi *Statement on Unity* (1961) begins with the relationship between 'all in each place' who share the Faith. The Gospel is clear on the Christian's relation with his neighbour, the person whom he does not choose but finds beside him, and whom he is commanded to love. Paul's letters are to Churches which consist of all who are in Christ in each place, and repudiate the idea of separate factions. It is such total groups, united for worship and led by one ministry, which represent the Church in their locality. Recognition of this situation, and their responsibility, is at the root of the parish system.

This system (though also used in secular administration) assumed the responsibility of a unified Church. The proliferation of divided denominations, each gathering its own flock, cuts

58

across it, a fact not removed by the practice of certain bodies, traditionally the settled Churches in particular areas, speaking of their parish, though in fact shepherding only their own people. Again, the sheer size of urban populations, and the artificiality of sub-dividing natural units to provide 'One Church, One Parish', have weakened it. On the other hand, co-operation and union of Churches have made it possible to visualize larger parishes, perhaps containing various congregations, sharing responsibility and working as a team for mission. Such a team properly consists not just of the ministers but of the whole Church membership.

The relevance of the parish is questioned from yet another angle, namely the conditions of modern life in which primary interests, decisions and relationships, may be at places of work, far from one's residence. It remains true that there is an inalienable significance in the 'place' where homes are made, childhood is spent, and people grow old and die. Yet these developments pose an urgent challenge to the Churches to look at their task in ways which must go beyond the old parish pattern.

[15, 31]

PIETISM (Piety; Pious): These words have fallen on evil days. A 'pious fraud' is a common, censorious phrase, and a 'pious opinion' one that leads to no action. One who is called pious may be dismissed as a religious humbug. Such usages represent the decline of a word whose basic meaning as 'dutiful and devout' still carries its proper significance in some contexts. Piety is the quality of one who takes religious duty seriously, and a Pietist is properly one marked by strong devotional feeling. Schools of devout Roman Catholics in the sixteenth century were so named.

Historically, however, Pietism was a powerful movement for

religious reform which arose, primarily among Lutherans, in the Germany of the late seventeenth century. It was associated with the names of Spener, founder of Halle University, and Francke, one of its first teachers. In a Church externally secure, theology had become highly intellectualized, concerned only to formulate correct Lutheran doctrine, and spiritual vitality was at a low ebb. It was then that Pietists who, like Christians (Acts 11: 26), Quakers and Methodists, got their name first as a nickname, sought to recover a living faith by promoting devout fellowship in small circles, emphasizing Bible study. To them faith was a matter primarily of the heart rather than the intellect, and in their judgement no one was qualified to teach Theology who had not a personal experience of regeneration. Stressing individual salvation and cultivating the spiritual life through fellowship, they sought to reconstruct a more primitive (N.T.) form of the Church, forming *ecclesiolae in ecclesia*. They were not, however, separatists, but generally stayed in the Churches, and, unlike mere Quietists, their piety led them to active philanthropy and a concern for foreign missions. The latter led to the Mission to Tranquebar in 1704, the real beginning of the Protestant missionary movement.

Puritanism is often, with some justification, associated with Pietism. Also stress on the spiritual to the neglect of other concerns has combined with it to create the familiar stereotype under which the Movement tends to be discounted. What is true is that lack of organizational control and emphasis on the individual opened the way for some fanatical, sectarian developments, which gave matter to the critics to use. Its Theology too was criticized, especially for its subjectivism. As a movement it ceased to be significant by the middle of the eighteenth century. Pietism, however, had lasting effects. It recaptured the significance of the saying: 'The heart makes the theologian', and Spener influenced Schleiermacher who was to deliver Theology from arid intellectualism. The modern missionary movement and Moravian origins owed much to it, and, through the Moravians, the awakening of John Wesley and so Methodism. Its permanent message is its stress on living faith and spiritual experience.

PRESBYTER (Presbytery; Presbyterianism): The Greek *presbyteros* (elder) either in full (presbyter) or shortened to priest, designates, in Episcopacy, the second of the three Orders of the Holy Ministry – ministers of Word and Sacrament, without the bishop's power to ordain. The earliest extant use of the term in this distinct sense is in the letters of Ignatius, who distinguished between the bishop and his presbyters (and deacons).

The distinction is not found in the N.T. where it is generally agreed that the terms refer to the same persons – elders in standing, overseers in function (Acts 20: 17 and 28). Nevertheless, since in N.T. times these functioned in churches in which the authority of the apostles was still available, to accept this view is not inconsistent with the theory that later bishops are successors of the apostles, not presbyters to whom special responsibilities have been given. Conclusive evidence to establish this theory, however, is lacking and the record of both Peter and John calling themselves *presbyteroi* renders it somewhat precarious (1 Pet. 5: 1; 2 John 1).

Presbyterianism is a form of Church government developed from a reading of the N.T. and later history which does not detect this essential difference of Order. It is noted that presbyters shared with apostles in Council (Acts 15: 23), were reminded of their episcopal functions (Acts 20: 28) and corporately laid on hands in Ordination (1 Tim. 4: 14) as a Presbytery (Greek *presbyterion*). It provides therefore for the collegiate responsibility and oversight (*episkopé*) of presbyters in each area.

In doing so it recognizes wider units than merely local congregations within the universal Church, and provides that Ruling Elders as well as ordained presbyters shall share in Church government.

The system provides for a hierarchy of Church courts. Of these the central one is the Presbytery, with equal numbers of ordained ministers and ruling elders in an area. Under the Presbytery, a local Session consisting of one minister and his elders is responsible in each parish. The Presbytery in turn is responsible to a higher court or courts (Synod and General Assembly) also composed of equal numbers of ministers and ruling elders. The Presbytery is the ordaining authority, the laying on of hands being by its ordained members. The President of each Church court is a minister, entitled the Moderator. In the Session he is the parish minister, in higher courts one selected to preside and to represent the court for a defined period.

Clearly there is considerable difference in status between a presbyter in this system, one of the single Order of the Holy Ministry, and a presbyter in a hierarchical Church, whose ordination does not include the ordaining power, here reserved to the Episcopate.

In other traditions, a presbytery is a place or building, either the eastern part of the chancel beyond the choir and sanctuary or (in Roman Catholicism) a priest's house.

[31]

39 **PRIEST** (Priestly; Priesthood; Sacerdotal): As a short form of presbyter the title denotes a clergyman whose ministerial functions include preaching, celebration of Sacraments, pastoral care of a congregation, and prayer with and for his people. None of this implies special privileges before God, or access to God which is denied to others. It does, however, include

a priestly ministry, shared by the whole Church, namely, that of representing God to others by making known the Gospel, and of representing others to God, especially by prayer. In this work, the Church fulfils the calling of the O.T. people of God, whom He who said 'all the earth is mine', named a 'kingdom of priests' (Exod. 19: 5f).

In this sense, priest translates the Hebrew *qohen* (Latin, *sacerdos* whence sacerdotal) and has a long history. The primitive priest was believed to have powers to make him an intermediary between men and the gods, or supernatural powers, capable of harming or helping men. Attached usually to a shrine, and thought to be specially near to its deity, he could be that deity's mouthpiece, or advise on how to propitiate it, or present for others the appropriate sacrifices. Traces of such ideas occur in the O.T., e.g. the story of one Micah who appointed a Levite as priest at his private shrine (Judges 17: 13), or priests brought to explain the ways of the Lord to new settlers in Samaria (2 Kgs. 17: 27).

In the O.T. the priestly office developed especially in relation to the temple and its sacrifices, with a growing insistence that the priest alone may offer sacrifice or burn incense at the altar (2 Chr. 26: 18) and the High Priest alone enter the Holy Place. The N.T., (Heb. 4: 14–16; 7: 23–28; 9: 11f, etc.) interprets the person and work of Christ as fulfilling this O.T. pattern of Priest and sacrifice, so that through what He has done 'once for all' we may 'draw near', knowing that He intercedes for us. Assured of what our Great High Priest has accomplished, the N.T. hints at no other individual priesthood continuous with that of the O.T., but the entire people is the new 'royal priesthood' (1 Pet. 2: 9).

The earliest sub-apostolic writings on the Eucharist describe the whole people as 'the offerers'. Soon, however, the precedent of the O.T. priesthood was quoted in writings on the Christian ministry. Later, as the Eucharist was interpreted as a propitiatory sacrifice the way opened to a conception of sacerdotal (priestly) control over the means of grace, which could be imposed by sanctions such as excommunication or an Interdict. This made possible such abuses as the sale of Indulgences, which finally precipitated the protest of the Reformation. It was such corruptions which brought even the words priestly and priestcraft into disrepute.

Against this background, the Reformation stressed the priesthood of all believers. The phrase, so far from denying priesthood, recognizes it in the whole Church, within which there is full place for those gifted, trained and ordained to preach and to minister to others. What is emphasized is that they do this, not in isolation, but within the full functioning of the Church, which is meant to reflect the ministry of our Great High Priest.

[31, 34, 44, 45]

40 **PROTESTANT**: In English this term is commonly used to designate those Churches which profess loyalty to the principles of the sixteenth-century Reformation and which, in Europe, are more often called Evangelical. It is today widely thought that the main principle involved is that of a right of private judgement, and the modern, negative meaning of the word 'protest' lends colour to this idea. Much more important, however, are the principles summed up in the Latin phrases, *sola scriptura* (by Scripture alone) and *sola fide* (by faith alone), of which the first indicates the authority by which doctrine is to be established, and the second the essential nature of salvation by grace through faith.

Historically, the term originated in the political Protest of a group of Lutheran Princes and cities at the Diet of Speyer (1529). This sought by a majority to reverse an earlier (1526) unanimous decision which had conceded the right of Princes to legislate, according to their conscience, in the light of Scripture, on religious matters in their respective territories. The Protest was a solemn assertion of this right which, it was averred, no subsequent Diet could, by mere majority vote, deny. The Princes concerned, and soon the Lutherans whose doctrines they upheld, became known as the Protestants. Later, at the Peace of Augsburg (1555) the legitimacy of their claim was conceded, securing a degree of recognition for these Protestants (Lutheran) which other Reformed groups did not enjoy. Only later was the term generally extended to cover these others.

In England, the word came to be used in this political, rather than doctrinal, sense to mark the claim by which the monarch's freedom was upheld to rule within her realm on religious matters. Consequently 'Protestant' designated the established Church, as distinct from Romanist and Puritan alike. This use of the term is preserved in such instances as the law safeguarding the Protestant Succession, the official title of the Protestant Episcopal Church in U.S.A., and in popular usage in Ireland.

Later centuries saw a shift in the secular use of the word 'protest' towards its current, rather negative, meaning. Further, those in Anglicanism who valued the Catholic heritage as against that of the Reformation, tended to repudiate the term, and, from the time of the Tractarian Movement, it came to be associated with a party position. In this context, the word suggests to its critics something negative, bare and sectarian, while its advocates would make it a militant banner under which to oppose a Churchmanship which they on their part repudiate.

Even without such militancy, there is a current usage which distinguishes Catholic, Orthodox, Anglican and Protestant Churches from one another. This, however superficially convenient, obscures the proper significance of each of these terms. Properly understood, they are by no means mutually exclusive.

[4, 26, 42]

41 PULPIT (Homily; Preaching; Pulpit and Altar Fellowship; Sermon): Ezra's wooden pulpit from which he read and expounded the Law (Neh. 8: 4) exemplifies the ordinary use of such a platform, particularly in Judaism, Islam and Christianity. The Christian pulpit is not for the exposition of personal opinions. From it the Scriptures are to be expounded, the Gospel proclaimed, the Faith taught and applied to life, all in the context of public worship, and forming the proper substance of sermons.

While such preaching has always been part of Christian worship, emphasis on it has varied much in history. It was highly esteemed in early centuries, with preachers of the calibre of Chrysostom, Ambrose and Augustine, the last of whom held that failure to preach, and thus to starve the flock, was no better than murder! Periods of neglect, when an ignorant priesthood was content to perform ritual acts, were offset by the rise of Preaching Orders like the Franciscans and Dominicans. Yet the Reformation found preaching in church at a low ebb, and its renewed stress on the Word led, not only to provision of Bible translations, but also to expository preaching which, particularly in the Reformed Tradition, became the central feature of public worship.

The position of the pulpit in church buildings partly reflects this history. Where the liturgy was emphasized, the chancel was reserved for the priests; and the pulpit, set up in the nave, was the place to which one of these might come to deliver a homily (simple exhortation) to the people. Where preaching was central, however, it might be placed centrally on the east wall, the Communion Table beneath it, though the fact that it is not the preacher who matters, but the Word which he serves, is emphasized by the custom of bearing a copy of the Bible into the pulpit before worship begins. Other buildings seek to express a balance between Word and Sacrament, with pulpit and lectern on either side and the Holy Table centrally between them.

The sermon is preached from the pulpit, and, in the Reformed Tradition, the whole service may be conducted from it. Located in a building used for Christian worship, it is rarely the place from which the Gospel today is heard by the outsider, so that proper evangelistic preaching is often heard from other platforms. Further, as it is normally used for uninterrupted discourse, ministers who wish to invite discussion, usually leave it to meet the congregation on another level.

The pulpit being for the authoritative exposition of Scripture and the Faith, Churches lay down rules as to who may occupy it. The title 'minister of Word and Sacrament' indicates that normally the same person is ordained to preach and to celebrate, though a licence to preach is sometimes given to a lay person whose appropriate gifts are recognized. In this context 'Pulpit and Altar Fellowship' is a phrase to indicate a relationship in which Churches reciprocally recognize their ministries, and are able to share both in preaching and sacramental worship, though here too invitations to the pulpit may be found where there is as yet no meeting at the altar.

[50]

REFORMED (Reformation): The Protestant Reformation of the sixteenth century was a complex movement, commonly traced to the stand taken in Martin Luther's 95 *Theses* published in October, 1517. Doctrinally it did not involve rejection of the Catholic Faith, set out in the Creeds, nor did rejection of papal claims imply repudiation of the Church, which the Reformers were generally agreed to recognize by the notes of the pure preaching of the Word and the right administration of the Sacraments.

State authorities adopted different attitudes to the movement in their territories, some supporting, others opposing it. This affected the forms of Church government which emerged in different areas, a variety sometimes accompanied by different doctrinal emphases, depending on the imprint of leading minds locally influential. Consequently, while the Churches had much in common, polity and doctrine varied, and generally they came to be categorized as either Lutheran (Protestant) or Reformed, the latter being associated with the teachings of Zwingli or Calvin. A third pattern emerged in England, mainly Reformed in doctrine, but more Lutheran in relations with the State.

Reformed Churches (e.g. in Scotland) tended to emerge from a popular movement where State authorities were unsympathetic. This favoured the search for a polity based on first principles (sought in Scripture) rather than from a previously existing structure. Following the Swiss example, this was generally Presbyterian. Here the further note of ecclesiastical discipline was added to those of Gospel preaching and the Sacraments to identify the true Church. These Churches were also marked doctrinally by an emphasis on the theme of Divine Sovereignty (*sola Dei gloria*) and the necessity of a well equipped Ministry of the Word.

Because of the controversies and with the lapse of time, the name Reformed could become associated with a new conservatism in doctrine, reflected today in the popular reputation of the Dutch Reformed Church in South Africa, or the small Reformed Presbyterian Church in Scotland. On the other hand, Reformed Churches generally, in official doctrinal statements, repudiate all claim to inerrancy, and declare their openness to further Reformation under the Word of God. This principle is summed up in the expression: *ecclesia reformata, semper reformanda* (reformed, always being reformed). While the decree of Vatican I on Papal infallibility emphasized what is irreformable, we may compare these words of Vatican II:

> Christ summons the Church, as she goes her pilgrim way, to that continual reformation of which she always has need, in so far as she is an institution of men here on earth.

Churches of the Reformed family formed in 1875 the World Alliance of Reformed Churches, a title now officially preferred to its alternative, the World Presbyterian Alliance, as expressing more accurately (and in line with the French and German titles) the position of its member bodies. This earliest of the World Confessional organizations has always kept its consultative character and has actively encouraged member Churches to enter into union with others.

[40, 50]

REPENTANCE (Penance; Penitence): Repentance, properly more than mere regret for misdoing, is a radical turning around, a moral reversal of direction: 'Turn back, turn back' (Ezek. 33: 11); 'Seek good, and not evil, that you may live' (Am. 5: 14f). Sometimes fear of judgement appears to be the motive, as when the Baptist warned men that the kingdom of heaven was at hand, and spoke of 'wrath to come' (Matt. 3: 2, 7), but the same message with Jesus sounds a positive note: 'Repent, and believe in the gospel' (Mark 1: 14f). Indeed the N.T. shows us repentance as a gracious gift of God for life (Acts 5: 31; 11: 18). That it is no mere emotion of regret or remorse is clear in the call for 'fruits that befit repentance' (Luke 3: 8), or a life befitting the new turning towards God (Phil. 1: 27; 1 Cor. 6: 11).

An evangelist's call for repentance and faith seeks to echo the N.T. proclamation with its assurance of forgiveness in Christ. There is a decisive character about acceptance, in the N.T. commonly associated with Baptism (Acts 2: 38) and some passages seem to exclude the possibility of further forgiveness for those who fall again into sin (Heb. 6: 4). However, the summons to Churches to repent (Rev. 2: 5), Paul's wrestling with his own and others' sin (Rom. 7: 24f; 1 Cor. 9: 26f) and his plea for the restoration of the penitent (2 Cor. 2: 5–10) point to a different conclusion. In fact, penitence, sorrow for sin as an offence against God, coupled with a genuine purpose of amendment, should mark the whole life of any Christian aware of his frailty. This is expressed in regular Christian worship, as it is in the Lord's Prayer. Our constant dependence on grace was stressed in Reformation theology.

The early Church, conscious of its stewardship of the Gospel (Matt. 16: 19; John 20: 23) faced the problem of the relation between forgiveness, associated with Baptism (Acts 2: 38), and post-baptismal sin. It developed a theology and practice of penance. An act of penance is properly an expression of repentance which also seeks, where possible, to make amends. The word came to be used for a full sacramental rite, in which the three elements of Contrition (penitence), Confession and Satisfaction open the way for Absolution pronounced by a priest. Confession, originally public, was later strictly private, while 'Satisfaction' is the word for prescribed acts of penance, which might include fasting, vigils, almsgiving, pilgrimage, etc. The whole rite is counted a Sacrament in the Roman Catholic and Orthodox Churches. In others, it is practised, with varying emphasis, within the pastoral 'cure of souls'.

The Greek and Hebrew words translated 'Repent' do express a radical turning, but the Vulgate Latin use of words meaning 'Do penance' led to an emphasis on the penitent's acts, which were popularly thought to earn merit. When it also became

70

possible to compound for these by money payments, the way to a corruption of the sacramental system was wide open. Luther's rediscovery of the Gospel of Justification by Grace through Faith, coupled with a recovery of the original Greek for repentance, brought a necessary corrective.

[1, 5, 13, 26]

SACRAMENT; The general idea of a Sacrament depends on the fact that spiritual experience may be stirred by physical events:

> ... a sunset touch,
> A fancy from a flower-bell, someone's death ...
> (Browning).

The Christian understands that it is God who thus makes material things even to be channels of His grace.

Some bodies (e.g. the Society of Friends), acknowledging this general sacramental principle and ready to see God's hand in any means which He may choose, yet refrain from particular religious rites. Others (e.g. Baptists) who practise Baptism and the Lord's Supper as ordinances of Christ prefer not to use the term Sacraments. Most Christian Churches, however, use the word (derived from the Latin *sacramentum*, a pledge) for certain specific rites, described by Augustine as 'a visible sign of a sacred thing'. Such signs, believed to have been given by Christ and used by His authority, do not just point to, or represent, spiritual reality. They are effective signs, instruments used by God to convey 'Christ and the benefits of the new covenant' to believers (*Shorter Catechism*). Calvin expounded this by speaking of the seal, the sign of authenticity which, standing alone, is without content, but attached to a document renders it operative. For this reason, he also stressed the relation between the

71

Sacraments and the Word which proclaims the Gospel of which they are the seal.

To be assured that a particular Celebration is valid, attention is given to what is done, how it is done, and by whom, areas of concern covered by the technical terms, Matter, Form and Minister. The Matter is the material used (water in Baptism, bread and wine in Holy Communion) and its use. This is important to ensure that the sign is indeed the one given by Christ. The Form is the words used to formulate precisely the intention of the act ('I baptize thee in the name of the Father, the Son and the Holy Spirit'). Celebration by a properly authorized (generally ordained) minister ensures that it is no mere private ceremony but an obedient act of the Church.

In early centuries the Church neither listed nor numbered the Sacraments (called in Greek the Christian Mysteries). The saying that they were 'many' is still taught in Orthodox circles. The Council of Florence (1439), however, confirmed what had become official teaching in the West, namely that they are seven, i.e. Holy Baptism, Confirmation, Holy Communion, Ordination, Penance, Holy Matrimony and Extreme Unction. These, under slightly different names, are commonly observed also by the Orthodox.

Of these Baptism and Holy Communion are widely accepted as dominical and 'generally necessary to salvation'. They are also called the Gospel Sacraments since in their content they express the whole redemptive work of Christ. These alone were recognized by the Churches of the Reformation as carrying the full authority of the Lord. Nevertheless, the other five, and indeed certain other rites as well, are widely acknowledged to possess a sacramental quality.

[5, 11, 26, 49]

SACRIFICE (Altar; Oblation): In common speech the word
means the surrender of something for the sake of a person or
cause counted more precious. Properly it refers to what is
made sacred by being surrendered to God. The altar is the Holy
Table on which such a gift to God is laid, and the gift is designated an oblation.

In many religions, sacrifices to gods or God are common, and
O.T. practice is no exception, though human sacrifice, familiar
in many primitive societies, is there uniformly denounced.
Sacrifices may be of grain, fruit or other possessions, but most
typically are of animals of which the life is offered to God. O.T.
sacrifices have different purposes: to express gratitude, to fulfil a
vow, to seal a covenant, to make good an offence, to ask a
favour, etc. They being regarded as prescribed by divine
authority, to offer them was an act of obedience. Their acceptance by God implied that He received the worshipper, and
the consequent Communion with Him was sealed in eating the
flesh of the sacrificed animal. A portion of it was burnt on the
altar, on which also was poured the blood (understood as
the life). Only the whole burnt offering, in expiation for sin, was
totally burned.

Properly sacrifices expressed spiritual devotion. What
prophets denounced was the blasphemy of making them a
substitute for, instead of an expression of, devotion (Isa. 1: 13;
Hos. 6: 6; Ps. 51: 17, etc.). Till N.T. times the system, with
daily sacrifices in the temple, continued and was used by many
to express humble devotion to God (cf. Luke 2: 22–24).

As a means for reconciling sinful man with God, sacrifice is,
in the N.T., seen fulfilled in Christ's self-giving for men. When
Paul teaches that He was 'put forward as an expiation by his
blood' (Rom. 3: 25) this is God's own gracious act to annul the
stain of sin (cf. also 1 Cor. 5: 7). The theme is developed in
Hebrews, where, stating that 'it is impossible that the blood of
bulls and goats should take away sins' (10: 4) the writer claims

F

that we have been 'sanctified through the offering of the body of Jesus Christ once for all' (10: 10). Hence the familiar words at Holy Communion 'pleading his eternal sacrifice'.

Grateful for what God has done in Christ, the worshipper is called to praise and to acts of generosity: 'for such sacrifices are pleasing to God' (Heb. 13: 16). Our proper response is 'to present your bodies as a living sacrifice . . . which is your spiritual worship' (Rom. 12: 1). That such a surrendered life has its focus in the Eucharist was seen in the early Church where worshippers who brought bread and wine for the service and for relief of the needy, were called offerers, and the widows and others helped were God's Altar!

The later doctrine of Transubstantiation, teaching that the substance of the elements was actually changed into Christ's flesh and blood, tended to a popular idea of the Communion as a propitiatory sacrifice, repeated on each occasion. While such teaching is not generally acceptable, there is a growing willingness to speak of the Eucharistic Sacrifice, where thanksgiving dominates, the once for all sacrifice of Christ is recalled before God, and the people offer themselves to Him in their 'spiritual worship'.

[11, 27]

46 **SYNOD:** This term is widely used for a properly constituted ecclesiastical assembly which meets to deliberate, advise or decide on questions of Faith and Order in the Church. It is used both for meetings specially convened for particular questions, and also for a regular organ in an orderly Church structure, to which specific powers are assigned.

In the first use of the term, no sharp distinction seems to mark it off from the alternative term, 'Council'. However, certain notable Synods have dealt with the resolution of divergencies, or the registering of agreements, between different bodies. This may reflect the root meaning of the word: a meeting of paths (from Greek *syn*, together, and *hodos*, a path). Examples are assemblies as varied as the Synod of Whitby (644) which brought the Celtic Church in England into conformity with Roman usage, the Synod of Diamper (1599) in Malabar, which temporarily did the same for the indigenous Syrian Church there, or the Synod of Dort (1618) where various national Churches of the Calvinistic Reformation reached a consensus on some doctrinal issues. In modern times, an outstanding Synod of this occasional character was that of Barmen (1934) when churchmen of both Lutheran and Reformed tradition adopted doctrinal Theses to oppose the Nazi threat to the Faith.

In the regular structure of the Churches, the use of the term varies according to constitutional provisions. Vatican II called for the setting up of a Synod of Bishops to assist the supreme Pontiff. Certain Orthodox Churches (e.g. the Russian) vest considerable powers in a Holy Governing Synod, representative of the whole. An Episcopal Church, like that of India, Pakistan, Burma and Ceylon, allots responsibilities to an Episcopal Synod consisting of Bishops and their assessors, reserving final decisions to a more widely representative General Council. In other Provinces of the Anglican Communion, a Provincial Synod has administrative powers for the whole area. It consists of the bishops with clerical and lay representatives selected according to agreed procedure.

In Presbyterianism, a Synod is usually a Church court, consisting in equal numbers of ordained ministers and Ruling Elders, with defined powers, intermediate between the local Presbytery and the General Assembly, the supreme court of the Church in a particular territory, e.g. the Church of Scotland. On the other hand, in Churches which have no such intermediate body, the term Synod may be used for the supreme court itself, e.g. the Synod of the Church of South India.

The phrase 'synodical government' generally represents application of the understanding that the Church is properly governed not so much by particular individuals, to whom authority is assigned, as by these as representative of the Church and its ministry, taking counsel together.

[16]

47 **TRADITION:** Basically a 'deposit', safeguarded and handed on, a tradition is a belief or custom passed on from generation to generation. Traditions may be local and limited in scope, or widespread and of ancient origin.

Christ condemned those who allowed 'traditions of men' to come in the way of obedience to God (Matt. 15: 1–9), and the Colossians were warned not to be misled by 'human tradition' (Col. 2: 8). Nevertheless, Christ did not reject all traditions (Matt. 23: 23) and the N.T. shows a Christian tradition emerging. Both regarding the Resurrection and the Lord's Supper, Paul claims to hand on what he received, even from the Lord (1 Cor. 11: 23; 15: 3). The Thessalonians also are to hold to the traditions they have been taught (2 Thess. 2: 15; 3: 6).

It is agreed that the apostles, as chosen witnesses of the Resurrection, were to transmit what they had seen and heard. This testimony is a sacred tradition. It is also agreed that the N.T. contains this Tradition, in written form, and used by the Holy Spirit to instruct the Church in later times. Questions emerge when that Church must later decide on doctrinal disputes. Here the bishops were generally accepted as the proper guardians of the Tradition, and not certain Gnostic teachers who professed to have a secret tradition from Christ. In Councils the bishops sought to formulate the Faith, always in harmony with written Tradition, especially on disputed matters. The fruit of their work, enshrined in the Creeds, is commonly held to be a

76

valid expression of the Tradition, reached by divine aid. However, since all statements must use language and thought-forms of their time there is an unceasing task of interpretation, in which new traditions grow. How far these are legitimate may be disputed.

The medieval Church saw the elaboration of teachings and practices which were justified by the claim that the bishops, as successors of the apostles, had access to an unwritten Tradition, entrusted to them. This was repudiated by the Reformers who held that Scripture alone provided the authentic record of the given Gospel. Against this, the Council of Trent claimed that the faith had been conveyed 'both in written books and in unwritten traditions, which were received by the apostles . . .' and called for 'equal veneration' for both. When Vatican I in 1870 laid it down that papal pronouncements *ex cathedra* are infallible, this made it possible for a later Pope (Pius IX) to claim: 'I am Tradition'! More recently, however, Vatican II has stated that '. . . sacred tradition, sacred Scripture and the teaching authority of the Church . . . are so linked and joined together that one cannot stand without the other'.

Orthodox Churches see Tradition as a living thing, used by the Holy Spirit, especially in the Liturgy, and accept it as a source of faith alongside Scripture. They deny, however, the possibility of any dogmatic addition to it without a genuinely Ecumenical Council.

Churches today generally recognize that they have developed traditions which call for constant appraisal in the light of what all have received. They agree that Scripture and Tradition must not conflict, and see the latter less as an inert commodity to be passed on and more as the total living experience of the Church.

[3, 16, 35, 42]

48 **UNITY** (Uniformity; Union): The conviction that Christians
who share one Faith should be recognizably at one is
related to the confidence that God is one, and that Christ is
the Universal Saviour. The confession, 'The Lord our God is one
Lord' (Deut. 6: 4) was seen by prophets to imply that the
world is His and will find salvation in Him (Isa. 45: 21f). This
is fulfilled in Christ: 'I, when I am lifted up from the earth, will
draw all men to myself' (John 12: 32). Consequently, those who
today seek Christian unity see its vital relation with the unity of
humanity.

In spite of the gulf then familiar between Jew and Gentile,
Peter's experience convinced the apostles that the way of
salvation is the same for both (Acts 15: 11). 'He is our peace, who
has made us both one' (Eph. 2: 14). In this publicly visible fact
'all men' may see the secret of God's unchanging purpose (Eph.
3: 9). That there is 'one body and one Spirit' (Eph. 4: 4) has led
Christians to confess their belief in 'One Holy Catholic Church'.

Paul was concerned that there be no division at the Lord's
Table (1 Cor. 11: 17f; Gal. 2: 11f), and in the second century
Ignatius saw the sharing of a single Eucharist under a single
bishop as the expression of the unity of the Church in each
place. Unity between local Churches was then expressed by
mutual acceptance at Holy Communion.

At this time the possibility of division within the Church was
not accepted. When a Church felt bound to exclude any from
fellowship it was in the sad conviction that these had betrayed
the Gospel and so had no place within the Body. Hence the
words: 'Let him be anathema' (1 Cor. 16: 22 AV). When, however, whole bodies differed and used the anathema against one
another, a new situation was created. Schisms began early, some
still unhealed, from the Councils of Ephesus (431) and Chalcedon
(451). Greek and Latin Churches were in schism from the
eleventh century, and the sixteenth-century Reformation saw a
further breach with Rome. Both Roman and Orthodox
78

Churches respectively clung to the belief that they alone were in each case the true Church, which had preserved unity while others had fallen away. Among others, mutual acceptance depended on Confessional agreement, though recognition of a place within the wider unity of the Body of Christ was not so circumscribed.

Disquiet over such divisions grew as Churches, independently organized, found themselves sharing the same territories, especially when involved in Christian mission in the wider world. In face of other faiths or no faith, they have been compelled to seek visible unity.

Their unity in Christ must seek expression. Some plead that 'spiritual unity' need raise no questions of polity, for those who differ may co-operate in some 'Federal Union'. Others, unable to evade the problem of mutual acceptability at the Eucharist, believe organic union to be essential. It is now seen, however, that complete uniformity in structure and liturgy is not requisite, but such recognition as will make possible a common life of worship and witness as the early centuries assumed, and as is expressed in an important Statement on the subject agreed by the W.C.C. at New Delhi in 1961.

[11]

VALID (Validity; Efficacy): In ordinary use, this adjective qualifies an argument which is logically sound or an action or document legally unassailable. In particular Churches it is so applied to an action, ordination or celebration which conforms to rule.

In Church usage, however, it has often carried a claim to reliability in the deeper sense that, the proper conditions having been fulfilled, such acts are assured of God's blessing and sure channels of His grace. This concept emerges in the teachings of

79

Ignatius who, seeking to build up orderly strength and unity in the Churches, laid it down that only those celebrations of the Eucharist are valid (Greek *bebaios*, reliable) which are under the authority of the bishop. This view, widely accepted, was strongly developed in the third century by Cyprian, who held that valid Sacraments could be celebrated only by validly ordained ministers, and that within the Catholic Church. With a wealth of O.T. quotations he argued that any Sacrament or ordination celebrated otherwise was a mere sham, incapable of conveying divine grace.

Even in Cyprian's time controversy arose about Baptisms by priests who were in schism from the Church. On his teaching these were totally void. Nevertheless, the practice prevailed by which persons so baptized were received without further baptismal service. The implication was that their baptism had been valid, though it was held not to have had efficacy as means of grace till the person concerned was within the Church's fellowship.

In the later Donatist controversy, this distinction between validity and efficacy was extended also to consecrations and ordinations, even in schism, by those who had themselves been duly consecrated. Augustine pled that these rites should not be repeated when one so ordained was later reconciled with the Church, though he also held that they lacked efficacy until this happened.

This view appears to underlie the later Roman Catholic attitude to the Orders and Sacraments of the Orthodox Churches, which they accept as valid, though irregular in having been given in schism from Rome. On the other hand, the Anglican Church has sought acknowledgement of the validity of its own Orders, and has examined those of others, in the conviction that such recognition implies recognition of Catholicity for the Church. This too is an inversion of Cyprian's approach.

Confidence in the validity of Orders and Sacraments has long been accompanied by humble acknowledgement that the divine grace may act outside these channels. The principle 'God is not bound to His Sacraments, but we are' has led to greater readiness in divided Churches to acknowledge that the reverent actions of other Churches may have efficacy, as true channels of God's grace, though they do not conform to our own rules of what is valid. Here, however, there is growing dissatisfaction with the term itself, with its apparently exclusive claims. Its implication of assured knowledge as to what may claim Grace and its negative implication for others undermine its general usefulness.

[8, 26, 34]

WORD (Bible; Scripture): The Ministry of Word and Sacrament concerns the means by which the grace of God is understood to be mediated in the Church. God's Word in biblical usage is His outgoing act, recognized in these forms: (a) His own commanding, creative Word (Gen. 1; Isa. 55: 11; Heb. 11: 3); (b) The message which came to the prophets and which they called on men to hear (Jer. 23: 29); (c) The proclamation of N.T. Evangelists (Acts 19: 20), which Paul sees as the divinely chosen means of salvation (1 Cor. 1: 21); (d) The Word made flesh in the Incarnation (John 1: 1–18), an insight which forbids us to identify the Word wholly with anything other than Christ, to whom the written or preached Word points; (e) The Bible as containing the authoritative record of what was given through prophet and apostle (2 Tim. 3: 16). So high a place is given to it that the Bible is sometimes even called 'The Word of God', though, more correctly, the Word is 'contained in the Scriptures . . .' for it is by the Spirit that the hearer may be quickened to recognize the message of God addressed to him.

The respect accorded to the Bible is shown in various branches of the Church by the reverent ritual to introduce its reading in some liturgies, by standing to hear it in others, or by the impressive ceremony with which it is placed in the pulpit of Reformed Churches. In the last of these, it is because the minister is primarily the servant of the Word, of which he is the ordinary expositor, that he presides also over the Sacraments. Reformed Theology has also been a Theology of the Word, an outstanding example being the work of Karl Barth. Further, the Reformation put the open Bible in men's hands, confident that through it the Holy Spirit would enlighten them. Since Vatican II, especially, Rome also encourages the faithful to study the Bible, while emphasizing the role of the Church as its interpreter.

Rome and Orthodoxy particularly point out that the Church determined which books should form the Bible. Reformed Churches, acknowledging this, point out that the bearer of a dispatch, capable of recognizing its authenticity by its seal, has no authority over its content, and see the Church as having been led to submit itself to the authority of Scripture. The Church indeed must always be open to reform under the Word.

Word and Sacraments express the same Gospel. Also celebration of a Sacrament involves the use of words to express intention. Care must therefore be taken to ensure that they are correct. When this is linked with religious conservatism, archaic terms and even a dead language may be retained, with a liturgy no longer understood, but the very sound of the words being thought to have power. However, Augustine's saying: 'Let the Word be added to the element and you have a Sacrament' is expanded with his reminder that the word is effective not because it is said but because it is understood. For this reason, the Reformers called for worship in the common tongue, and Vatican II has encouraged vernacular renderings of the Liturgy of the Mass.

[4, 26, 41]

INDEX
[of terms not separately treated]
The reference is to the number of the article